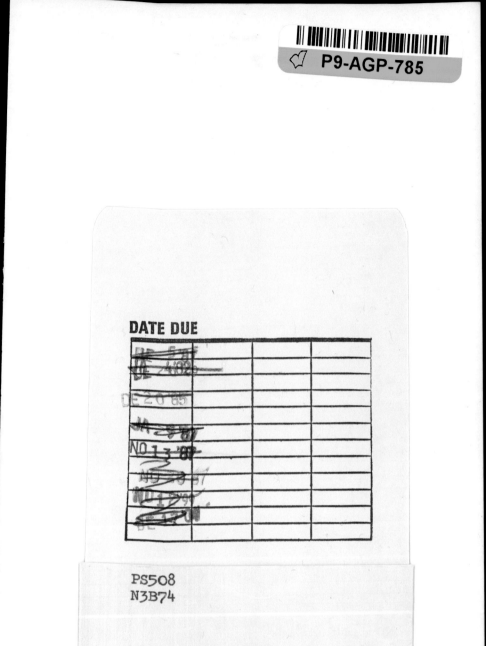

P9-AGP-785

DATE DUE

PS508
N3B74

RIVERSIDE CITY COLLEGE
LIBRARY
Riverside, California

JUL   1980
DEMCO

JUMP BAD

JUMP BAD

A New Chicago Anthology

Presented By

GWENDOLYN BROOKS

bp

BROADSIDE PRESS

12651 Old Mill Place, Detroit, Michigan 48238

Riverside Community College
Library
4800 Magnolia Avenue
Riverside, CA 92506

PS508.N3 B74 1971
Brooks, Gwendolyn,
1917-2000.
Jump bad; a new Chicago
anthology.

First Edition

Second Printing, December 1972

Copyright © 1971 Broadside Press

No part of this book can be copied, reproduced, or used in
any way without written permission from Broadside Press,
12651 Old Mill Place, Detroit, Michigan 48238

Cover by Cledie Taylor

LCN: 79-126925
ISBN: 0-910296-32-2

Manufactured in U.S.A.

DEDICATED TO HOYT FULLER,
GREAT EDITOR—WARM EDUCATOR

CONTENTS

INTRODUCTION

In May of 1967 Oscar Brown Jr. introduced me, via telephone, to Walter Bradford. Walter Bradford was to gather for me the literary-minded among the Blackstone Rangers, a huge collection of Chicago black youth. Awed by a preview of "Opportunity, Please Knock," a brilliant musical show developed by Oscar out of Ranger talent, I had asked if there were not poets and prose-writers among the hoofers and singers. The reply was a quick Yes. And this Walter, who knew and understood teen "gangsters" very well, who had been for long a teen organizer, was to be my gatherer.

That was an unforgettable voice—young, clean, strong; bracing, male, reliable; confident, but warm; not afraid to be friendly. When I met its owner I found him proud, but not too proud to aid, pleasantly, a sallying middle-aged woman who thought she knew what she was doing but did not know what she was doing. Gradually, as gradually the Rangers drifted back to their rehearsals which (in the First Presbyterian Church on the South Side) were going on directly *above* the sobrieties of our creative writing class, Walter introduced to me other talented youth organizers of his acquaintance, and students from Wilson, the college he attended. (Later, I urged Walter to create a creative writing class of his own, from among the Rangers, and he did so, eagerly and meticulously; he had a class of about twenty no-nonsense young fellows who, with an eager meticulousness of their own, arranged chairs, maintained order, and afforded him their strict attention.)

The "older young" were at once wary and curious. Alicia Johnson, Jim Taylor, Mike Cook, Peggy Susberry. Don Lee, who had already published "Think Black" and who is now the most significant, inventive, and influential black poet in this country. Sharon Scott, our one high-schooler. Came also Kharlos Tucker, who is now Sigmonde Wimberli, Ronda Davis, Jewel Latimore, who is now Johari Amini, Jim Cunningham, Carolyn Rodgers, Doris Turner, Carl Clark.

With the arrival of these people my neatly-paced life altered almost with a jerk. Never did they tell me to "change" my hair to "natural." But soon I did. Never did they tell me to open my eyes,

11

to look about me. But soon I did. Never did they tell me to find them sane, serious, substantial, superseding. But soon I did.

I am proud of these young people. Most of them are in their twenties, with Sharon, the youngest, now only nineteen, and *sixteen* when I met her.) They scratch out roads for themselves, are trying to BE themselves. They do not mind making "mistakes." In a new nation, what *are* the mistakes, anyhow? What are the cliches? what are the offenses against standards? What are the standards? Who decides? Are the rulers of *other* nations to decide?

Incidentally, the question of my status, my position, (was I or was I not a Teacher, a Workshop Ruler?) was soon a gentle joke. I "taught" nothing. I told them, almost timidly, what I knew, what I had learned from European models (well, Langston Hughes too!) And they told me without telling me that the European "thing" was was not what they were about. "Iambic pentameter," they twitted. "Hmmm. Oh yes, iambic pentameter. Well, now . . . " Eventually I gave up imposing exercises—and we became friends. We discussed Issues, we read our work to each other, sometimes criticizing, sometimes not. We respected and liked each other, in spite of occasional attitude clashes. The first and unifying thing we understood about each other was that we were, all of us, Black. Not "Negroid," but Black. The second thing we recognized was that we all most anxiously "wanted to write."

Many of these black writers are now involved in an exciting labor, a challenging labor; admitting that it is not likely all blacks will immediately convert to Swahili, they are blackening English. Some of the results are effective and stirring. Watch for them.

True black writers speak *as* blacks, *about* blacks, *to* blacks.

Further. These black writers do not care if you call their products Art or Peanuts. Artistic Survival, appointment to Glory, appointment to Glory among the anointed elders, is neither their crevice nor creed. They give to the ghetto gut. Ghetto gut receives. Ghetto giver's gone.

Sig gives us his Denmark Shabazz, his Sojourner Bethune!

GWENDOLYN BROOKS

SIGMONDE WIMBERLI
(Kharlos Tucker)

Fear Came Early

They lynched Jimmy Olds when I was eight, four years before my first erection. But I wasn't really scared. I knew it was going to happen. My grandfather told me he had heard the white folks talking up in town. They were standing around getting all liquored up, some were whooping and jigging about, in anticipation of "teaching the niggers a lesson ternight."

I couldn't see why they would lynch Jimmy. All he'd done was kiss a white girl. Some folks even say it was the white girl who kissed Jimmy. White girls had kissed me too, but not on the main street on a Friday evening. They had put him in jail across the street from our house, and I had taken him some dinner and some Kool Aid before they came and took him up town. He was crying, and saying he didn't want to get whipped, at least not out in front of everybody like they told him they were going to.

13

He wasn't even tied up when the sheriff put him in the back of the pick-up and headed toward town. He just had the handcuffs on. I wanted to ride uptown with him, but my grandfather wouldn't let me, and cuffed me across the head, when I wouldn't stop asking.

The sun was almost down; I was anxious to go up town and see Jimmy get whipped and get it over with. We was supposed to steal some cantaloupes from ol' mister Whittler's melon patch that night and ride our bikes out to Minnie Lou and Gladys Jean's house in the country. They sure liked cantaloupes. And they was showing me what to do when I got my first hard on. Jimmy Lee was already busting his nuts, and I could hardly wait until I could. But I would let Gladys Jean put my "thing" in her big mouth and suck it while Jimmy and Minnie Lou were down on the ground screwing for real.

By the time me and my grandfather got to town, everybody else was there. I had had to sit on the porch and watch while most of the black people passed by, and I secretly called my grandfather the "slowest ol' bastard in the world."

Jimmy Lee was already getting whipped. They had him tied to the back of a wagon, and Rudy the blacksmith was swinging a wide leather strap with holes in it. It hummed through the air and cracked like a rifle when it hit Jimmy Lee's back. He was sceaming at first, but by the time I got up close enough to see good, he was just shaking like a tired hound everytime Rudy hit him with the strap. The white folks were yelling to Rudy to hit him harder and Rudy's grunts proved he was doing his best to please.

Pretty soon they untied his arms and laid him in the gravel on the road. The sheriff got up and began to talk about what a fine warning they had given to the "colored people" in the town, and how they hoped this would convince them they should keep their "young bucks from sniffing 'round liddle white gurls."

I still wasn't scared when they picked Jimmy up off the street and dumped him in the hot tar, then yanked him out and dumped the feathers all over him. But I shook a little inside when they dragged him down the street behind that pick-up truck. I knew how that felt. Jimmy Lee had started screaming again, and I put my hands over my ears. I felt like cheering when the chain came aloose, but something in the mood of the other black kids warned me not to. They were all very silent and staring wide-eyed while Jimmy Lee was being dragged up and down the street.

I did cheer though, when Jimmy Lee got up and tried to run. But they caught him before he could get more than a few steps away. One of the rednecks wearing a loud shirt and cowboy boots ran up to him and threw a rope around his neck. Then he and some of the others dragged him back to the wagon where they had been whipping him. They threw the end of the rope over one of the lamp posts and pulled on it until Jimmy's feet were off the ground.

I was getting mad then. I didn't see no need to hang him from that lamp post. All he did was kiss a little old white girl. And she was so ugly everybody called her "frog," even the white kids. She was fat, and wore thick glasses and had big blackheads all over her face. But they kept pulling on the rope until Jimmy Lee's feet were higher than a grown man's head.

I knew Jimmy Lee must have really been hurting. I had got my tie caught in a car door one time, and I never forgot it. I was hoping they would let Jimmy Lee down in time for us to go steal the cantaloupes and get out to Minnie Lou and Gladys Jean's house. We could get the tar and feathers off with turpentine and we could put some of my grandfather's soap-'n-axle grease salve on the places that was all scratched up real bad. But we had to hurry and get out there before their daddy got back from town. Otherwise they couldn't get out of the house after dark.

Then I saw them making up the fire again. They piled up some more cross-ties from the railroad yard and threw some gasoline on them. The fire jumped up in the air under Jimmy Lee and then I saw his eyes all popped out and his tongue hanging out of his mouth like a tired hound. I was getting madder all the time. If they didn't hurry up and let him down he was going to choke to death and I would be too scared to steal ol' man Whittler's melons by myself. And if Jimmy Lee wasn't with me, I didn't want to go out to Minnie Lou and Gladys Jean's.

The shooting made me duck, even though I was way down in our section of town, and I saw they were shooting up in the air at Jimmy Lee. But we could see as good as the white kids up on their end, because the fire lit up the whole two blocks of Main Street.

15

I knew, after they shot him, that Jimmy Lee was hurt bad, and we wouldn't be going to steal any melons or out to Minnie Lou and Gladys Jean's. But I though they had done enough to him already for just kissing a girl. And I wondered why they didn't let him down so his mother and father could take him home and get all that tar off him and put some salve on all them scratches and holes. They might could have gotten ol' Doctor Nickels to come out to see him, and do something about them gunshot wounds.

His momma was sitting in the wagon crying real loud and his daddy was holding her in his arms. She kept jumping up trying to get out of the wagon, but he wouldn't let her. She kept telling him she wanted to go and get Jimmy Lee and take him home. His daddy said they couldn't till the white folks got through with him.

But they never let Jimmy Lee come to the wagon. When they untied the rope and let him down, he fell right next to the fire. While he was lying there, I asked his daddy could we keep Jimmy Lee at our house so we could go to Sunday School together in the morning. His daddy didn't say nothing. My grandpa told me to hush up. The white folks were starting to leave. The colored folks weren't moving. It seemed like they were frozen in one spot. I was getting sleepy and told my grandpa I was ready to go home and go to bed. He told me to hush up.

That's when the two Wilson boys picked up Jimmy Lee and threw him in the fire. His momma screamed and tried to jump out of the wagon again. Jimmy Lee's daddy grabbed her. I called to Jimmy Lee to get up and come over where we were, but didn't nobody go down the street to pick him up out of the fire. They just stood and watched.

I asked his daddy why he didn't go get Jimmy Lee out of the fire, and before he could answer, my grandpa backhanded me in the mouth and I went sprawling to the ground. I started crying real loud so my grandmother would hug me up and kiss the tears away. But she didn't this time. She just gritted her teeth and hissed at me to shut up before she went and got a switch and gave me something to really cry about.

The smell made me and some of the other kids vomit. It was the first time I had ever smelled a person burning up.

After all the white folks had gone away, we all walked up and looked at what was left of Jimmy Lee. The older folks tried to keep the kids away, but we ducked around and through legs and looked anyway. The men helped his daddy put Jimmy Lee in the wagon. He was all dried up and crusty all over, and about half as big as he had been.

When we got into our yard, I asked my grandpa if we could see Jimmy Lee in the morning since he was too sick to come to Sunday School. He stooped down and picked me up and set me on the porch bannister and told me Jimmy Lee wasn't ever going to Sunday School again, but that we could go to his funeral. He seemed a little puzzled when I asked him how he knew for sure Jimmy Lee was going to die. But he explained to me that all those things that the white people did to Jimmy Lee had already made him dead, and just like guessing the next question on my mind, he told me that white people always do that to a colored boy when they catch him touching a white girl the wrong way. He told me how sometimes they even cut off a boy's "thing," I really got scared then. The fear leaped through my body and I started to shake all over. Cut off my thing! I hadn't even busted my nuts for the first time yet.

I couldn't sleep all night. I stayed awake wondering if they were going to come and get me out of the house and do those things to me that they had done to Jimmy Lee. I got out of the bed and stayed on my knees a long time, asking God to please keep the little Wilson girl from telling her brothers what we'd been doing.

Every day after school we had been sneaking down in the weed patch and taking off our clothes and playing with each other all over. I would put my finger up in her little hole and she would pull on my thing and roll my balls around in her fingers. I was so terrified I sweated and prayed all night. And every little noise was as loud as thunder in my ears. Every time a dog barked I jumped under the bed, just knowing "they" were coming into the yard and up on the porch and into the house without knocking . . . just like they had done at Jimmy Lee's house. I got my whittling knife out of my pocket and opened it and put it between the mattress. I swore I would stab the first hand that reached under the bed after me.

And I almost got my neck broken when my grandfather attempted to pull me out that morning. I had fallen asleep with the weapon clutched in my hand. When he came in at daybreak to send me out to get the eggs and milk the cow, I was not in the bed. Noticing a foot sticking out, he proceeded to drag me from beneath the bed. I awoke in the tight terror that had kept me awake most of the night, and jabbed the blade into his hand. He thought I had hidden to keep from going out to do the chores and had bitten his hand. He yanked me out by the foot and my chin caught on the bed railing, nearly taking my head off and making me dizzy.

Before he could upright me into position for his terrible backhand in the mouth, I managed to blurt out I was hiding from the white men. Thinking it was a bad dream, he told "wasn't no white men cummin'" to get me and I had better get my little self out and do my chores. Before he could get out of the room, I told him Mary Jo Wilson and I had been playing with each other out in the weed patch. He stopped and looked at me and opened his mouth to say something, then closed it, and after a long while, told me to come and tell him and grandma about it. I followed him into the kitchen where I repeated for my grandmother what I had told him, only more in detail. They told me to go out and do the chores, but to come straight in the house when I finished.

Instead of being on the way to Sunday School at 9:15, I was on my way to the city to catch the train for Chicago. I was scared for a long time that they would find me and take me back for my whipping.

MIKE COOK

Bootie Black and the Seven Giants All Sipping Chili (Benign) to the Tune of Gertrude Stein Polishing the Knob of Crip Heard

All in a literary parleur
Within sight of a certain voyeur

namely, the ghost of Melvin Tolson

"Hee hee" said this revenant, "hee hee"
and did a cartwheel, and then split.

"Oh puhleeze, please" says your Artiste
pleading for spatial and syntactic integrity
before the onslaught of spirochete anew

and before being inundated in lawn ordure
and before being impaled by the spear cast
of a cold and alien moon.

And she said "If you don ack right, Roscoe,
I'm not gon do you no mo favors."
And that was a long time ago!

And you dreamed, did you, that you were married to a duck?
And now you find that you're quacking, too?
And you quack at me to come and save you from your duckdom!
Your eyes must surely tell you that I don't dig that song too swell.

Strange African chicks, strange island chicks
Who will stick beside even the most garishly bedecked brother
With even the strangest expression on his face.

The specific gravity of the Black skelton
Is 1.06 times that of the white skelton.

And we try to sleep on a soft narrow couch.
And it's only the first time that we've screwed.
And it's not particularly pleasant outside.
And yet you say that you must go?
Yes, you must go.

If I Knock You Down, Don't Blame It On Me

The secretary knew his name because there weren't but two of them in the company and the other one, Mac, was six-nine and weighed 295. "Hello, Harry. Mr. Formalder will be with you right away. The account exec from Leo Burnette is in there now."

He was supposed to talk, but he wasn't in a good mood. All he said was, "Oh yeah?"

She didn't notice that he was curt and his nose was in a magazine. "Don't mention it, but I think Formalder isn't happy and our account might be going somewhere else." She probably wouldn't have told anyone but him. Or Mac! That was different. They were the repositories of secrets.

"Harry, Don, you two guys ever met? No? Harry Devlin, Don Jenkins! Yeah, that's great fishing. God, those Marlins! Harry, you ever fish, for real, like down in Florida? No, you don't fish, Harry doesn't fish. Harry doesn't fish for fish, anyway. Ha, ha, ha! What about lunch sometime next week, Don? O.K., see you, fella. Come on in, Harry. Harry, baby, how's everything going?" And there was his smile, which alternated with his studied gravity; all done laboriously with little, tired muscles around his mouth.

"Fine, Phil. How's everything with you?"

"Problems, Harry. Problems and problems." And he ducked his head and smiled a forgiving smile. "I guess you're here to talk about that district managership, huh? Well, have a cigar."

"No thanks, Phil. You're still smoking those cheapies." And Harry pulled a long, thin Brazillian cigarillo from a plastic case and lit up.

"I don't know why we can't get right down to facts, Harry. You know I met with the Big Boys down in Miami last week. It wasn't felt that you're the man for the job."

Harry leaned back in the leatherine chair and blew smoke. He stretched his legs out. For a few seconds he watched Phil Formalder drum his fingers and fiddle with a manila folder. "Why not?"

"Well, Harry, you've met them and they've met you. They know what they want. And frankly, while we're levelling, you've never exactly come off to them as a company man. Now, nobody's knocking your sales or customer satisfaction or anything like that. That's

just the impression they've got of you. Hell, you know the mysti-
que of the business world, Harry."

Harry took another long pull and blew the smoke up at the
ceiling. He studied the Picasso harlequin. He leaned in close to
Phil, both elbows on Phil's desk. "That's crap, Phil, and it's starting to really stink."

"I've got your entire folder here, Harry. You know, we started
not to hire you at all. Your test and background didn't really fit in
with what we wanted. But you've got a lot else going for you.
Hell, everybody knows that. Listen, Harry, do you think I'd come
back from Miami empty-handed? Listen, kid, there was a guy from
the Federal Equal Opportunity Commission down there. We talked to him and we're going to have a guy represent us to colleges
and high schools on a full-time basis. And not just the black
schools, either. And who do you think we've got in mind?"

Phil smiled again, hard, really working at it. And Harry remembered the couple of times he had had occasion to see Phil really
tomming, and being fascinated at the refinement and depths, the
shamelessness. "It's a great deal, Harry. You'll have a lot of auto-
nomy and you'll be conferring with the guys in Washington. Uncle
Sugar's subsidizing some of the expenses and salary." Phil hunched
up close to Harry to mention the salary figure. Harry moved the
cigar. Phil peered in close like a fish staring out of a bowl. His
eyes pierced the lacquer for the first time during the interview.
This was the part Phil liked. He whispered the salary.

But Harry was thinking about that Hip student teacher he had
in high school who turned the class on to films; and the time he
took him and three others to Maxwell Street and then over to the
Greek market and shot a lot of old people; and the short film he
had made about the dreams of a junkie that won second prize at
the college film festival; and the really hilarious shit that him and
that Jewish lieutenant managed to sneak into that Army training
film, telling the GI's what to do if furtive Europeans and pretty
girls with accents approached them; and the film about the tenor
player stranded in Paris that he had wanted to make with that
rich, Swedish cat's bread.

"Who's going to get the district managership?"

"It wasn't like that, Harry. Nobody's lined up for that yet. Besides, it would take a blind man not to see that the Equal Oppor-

tunity Representative is best for you. How about it? We'd like to start you off on that as soon as possible."

"I'll let you know, Phil."

"When?"

Harry was getting up then, stretching. He was sorry he had brought his briefcase, now that he wasn't going to do any work. "Monday or Tuesday, Phil. Or Wednesday or Thursday. Have a nice weekend."

It was Friday, and Daddy-O was playing an old Coleman Hawkins Cut. It was one of the first warm days of the year. It was noon. The growly tones of the master cleaned Harry's mind like good cocaine clears the nasal passages, and he wheeled the Pontiac off the Outer Drive at 47th Street and headed for the Trocadero. There was a good crowd, and King Kolax had just come off the stand.

"Harry D. My Man."

"Bo, Bo baby. Long time, long time."

"Too long, Jack. Come on out of here and let me get you high." They walked around the corner and smoked and got high and Harry remembered the staunch companions of hot, summer Saturdays and the porch-side nine-year old fist-fights and the forays down Dead Canyon in search of white boys to fight. Bo, the first to go to reform school. "You remember that time Mr. Huber caught you forging that note for me? Your father came and got you back in the next day, but I went to Monty-fee. But it wasn't no big thing. I came back. I remember the only time you got caught was the time we broke that Dude's window that Halloween. How did you let that old dude catch you, anyway?"

"It was a real funny thing, Bo. It was like a nightmare thing, and I was running hip deep in molasses. He beat the shit out of me, too. Why didn't you and Scrounge come back and help me?"

" You was too far behind us, and you had no business getting caught, really. You hip to that? And what was that you used to always say, huh? Remember? 'if you see me fighting a bear, motherfucker, you help the bear,' remember?"

But who, really could fight like Bo? or run as fast as Isaac, dance with two broads like Sonnyboy? Or signify like Romeo whose eye, worse than any schoolyard bully's, sought you out as he wandered from victim to victim; and you could hang back, hoping

23

to avoid his eye, or toady up in his face. It was all useless.

Back in the club, King Kolax resumed the stand (as the other band hadn't shown yet). King was old, and his trumpet sometimes wavery, but he was always down enough to have young sidemen who were listening to the latest stuff. True to this, his piano player and tenor men were where it was at. King himself was playing well. The crowning touch was the left-handed, blues guitar player with the speed and technique that stopped the tinkle of glasses and undertone murmur of the crowd. The contrasts were pleasing to Harry—the young musicians and old, jazz and the blues.

As a treat for his eye, Harry looked across the table at Bo's companion: Carmel, 16 years old, black, and half oriental. As she sipped scotch, she told of her recent escape from the State Training School for Girls. The room seemed properly crowded, properly smoky, properly intimate. Harry knew people: some by name, some by face, some by reputation.

Percy and Leena came in. Percy had lived in those raggedy bungalows east of Wentworth rather than in the projects, and so had belonged to the Sharks rather than the Rangers. Leena had always liked Harry. In the boots and grime of a construction worker, and the grin of an antagonism grown amiable with time, Percy made himself and his lady comfortable, and helped himself to Bo's liquor. "You two dudes still runnin' together, huh? Old Bo and Harry D! You still writin' bad checks, Bo? You still downtown jivin,' D?"

Bo answered, "Bighead Motherfucker, when are you going to learn to be nice and polite?"

Harry's gaze and Leena's returned smile focused onto one hot, Chicago summer afternoon eight years before, casual (or how could it be when they had already known each other ten years) and inevitable and frightening. Like doing it to his first cousin. "You look awfully pretty, lady."

"Is that all you can say after all these years?" And she laughed the same laugh, like a light, inspired run on the vibes.

"You've changed so little it frightens me."

"I've got three babies now, you know."

"Seems like I missed a lot."

"You know what you missed."

"D, get your liver-lips out of my lady's ear."

24

"Damn, Percy," said Bo. "Old friends can't talk without you going into your act. What's wrong with you?"

Carmel had been following the exchanges with intense interrest. "All youall friends, huh. All youall from 95th St. What's your sign, Percy?"

"Taurus."

"What's your sign, Harry D?"

"Pisces."

"What's your sign, Lady?"

"Aries."

"Well, I know what happened, now." And she nodded her exquisite and beautiful face.

Harry left the Trocadero, got in his car, headed east to the Drive and then to South Shore. His mood was right for his mission; a visit with his son, brief financial transaction with the mother.

There is the funny feeling of coming into the home that isn't yours anymore. The eye wanders unbecomingly, even under discipline; looking for, oh, you name it—a cigarette filter of an alien brand, a pair of slacks hanging in the closet, should one weaken enough to look; any number of signs, things. But in the case of this visit, the artifact itself sat comfortably, stockingfooted, clutching a beer.

"Harry, I'd like for you to meet Felix."

"Ah yes, really my pleasure, old chap," said Felix. "I've heard so much about you."

"Felix was at Michigan State at about the same time you were at Michigan, Harry."

"Is that right? Not likely we'd have met, though."

"Not likely at all, old boy. East is East and West is West and all that sort of Tommyrot."

"What's your last name, by the way?"

"I'm really afraid you couldn't pronounce it."

"Oh no?"

"Harry, would you like a beer?"

"Yes, and would you call the kid, please?"

"Emmy tells me you are a salesman, if I remember right."

"That's right."

"Yes, yes, tha't in the right direction. It seems to me that so many of you American Blacks wind up in services. And who, by and large, are you servicing? Ha, ha, ha!"

"Yeah, well, you know all about it. You'll be taking your expertise back home, no doubt. Where is home, by the way?"

"Felix is from Nigeria, Harry, and right now he is working on his doctorate in economics at the University of Chicago. There's Daddy Harry, Poogie. Say Hello!"

"Hello there, Big Boy. Whatcha been doin' today?"

"Playin'."

"You go to Kindergarten today?"

"Yes, I go every day except Saturday and Sunday."

"Now, we're going to the zoo tomorrow, right?" Blank look.

"You told him, didn't you, Emmy?"

"I guess I forgot, Harry."

"Well, anyway, Big Boy, how would you like to go to the zoo tomorrow?"

Big smile, "O.K."

"All right, I'll be by for you in the morning, and we'll check out some of those bad beasts of the jungle, like lions and tigers and anaconda snakes. You ready for 'em?"

"Yeah, I'm ready for 'em. What's an anaconda snake?"

"That's one, my boy, that if he's hungry and he gets a chance to wrap himself around you, he'll crush the livin' bejesus out of you, right down to a convenient bite-size morsel. Am I right, Felix? Tell him about those bad beasts of the jungle."

"All that you say and more, my friend."

"Be ready in the morning, Poogie. Be ready."

Fridays seemed better to Harry than Saturdays. It was Friday that he associated with the really good music, the good parties, the end of good projects. Saturdays were mixed up with irresolution and the wrong kinds of people. Still well within Friday, he reached Dali's apartment.

"Ha-aary, you're la-aate." But he got a kiss, anyway.

"I'm not in a hurry anymore. What you got to drink? And eat?"

"Oh, Harry! I thought we were going to eat out and then go to the Pomegranate Room." But, good girl and loving woman that she was, she put the pot on. Harry shaved and showered, and they dined on lamb chops, mushrooms, eggplant and a salad with black olives and gorgonzola cheese.

"Baby, I'm going to lay down for just a minute." He put on a stack of sides with Archie Shepp's "In A Sentimental Mood" first. He stretched out, thinking that perhaps all he had ever learned about women was that the size of the bed in a single woman's apartment is usually enough to tell you what time it is. He dozed and dreamed of the big blizzard, and him walking through the snow with a girl, both high on LSD, and winding up at the sissy bar on 51st Street and listening to the long-head preacher talk of Somerset Maugham.

She shook him, "Harry, Harry, it's time to go," and he came awake and his hand split her robe and planed from the waistband of her panties to the nape of her neck. He buried his hand in her hair and ran his mouth and tongue around and in her ear, and using his teeth at the beginning of her hairline and where her neck joined her shoulder. She turned on her back and they took off her robe. "Feed me," and with one hand she cupped her breast and with the other pulled his head towards her. Her back arched as he described a circle around her nipple with his tongue and mustache, arched harder as the gargle in her throat changed to a hiss as he sucked the nipple in. Her legs went up and he was listening to her voice as she called him and called him and marvelling at her voice and at the both of their voices as they were joined.

They got to the Pomegranate Room and the spectral master of ceremonies, Benny, was in charge; eyes seemingly closed, staring through his lids into the mood of the audience—an M.C. who had paid all the dues. He was in charge. Harry's friend, Rita the Magnificent Chanteuse, sang her song that goes, "If You Can't Drive, Get Out of the Driver's Seat." At the close of the set, Rita visited with Dali and Harry.

Harry: Sweetheart, you are in Magnificent voice.
Dali: Rita, Baby, you are taking care of business tonight.
Rita: Glad you liked it. I am in good form tonight, aren't I?
Harry Oh yes. Cognac for the chanteuse—drinks for everybody.

The band members stopped by and Harry went out with the tenor man, The Commodore (who, like all other tenor players, the higher he was the more he sounded like Lester Young) to get high. On returning, Gino had joined the table; Gino being perhaps the hippest white boy left on the South Side. The hippest white boy left, anyway, in this the age of the eclipse of the junkie; although that whole thing is an interesting scene. Terry Southern described a razor fight and choreographed it like they were two Russian ballet dancers who just happened to be cutting each other to death. Some real 'code duello' shit and it even fooled a couple of white acquaintances who usually know what's happening.

"Hello, Harry."

"Hello Gino." Harry sat down and patted his girl on the butt. The Commodore led the band into an Illinois Jacquet type thing and strolled off the stand, horn blasting as he pivoted and turned, giving each table the full bell and letting them hear a horn player in his full power. Benny then took the stand to exercise his special crowd magic. He looked as if he were being held erect by the spotlight on his face, illuminating the agony of the old skeletons raging in his veins. Rita took the stand and sang. While she sang songs, she sang of herself; and of old lives left in San Antonio and St. Louis and New York. "Oh that chick can sing. She can really sing."

"Yeah I'm her manager now. Or didn't you know?" Gino postured, and the full image suddenly occurred to Harry: Bob Steele playing Curly in the movie "Of Mice and Men.. and telling all about his vaselined glove.

"Let's go, Dali."

"Soon as I finish my drink, Harry."

"Yeah, Harry, damn. Let this fox finish her drink. You want to remove this star and ruin everybody's evening. The drinks are on Gino tonight. Let's party. Let's party real good. Why don't you all come by my place from here? We'll party real good. It'll be a real select crowd and some real select action."

"Oh Harry, let's go by Gino's."

"No. Let's split. It's late." Harry stood up.

In the condensed time that Dali didn't move, Gino spoke in his soft voice, his trademark, "Baby, you really don't have to go if you don't feel like it."

"Gino, don't you know that when you're a bad boy like that you're liable to get a foot up your ass?"

"Ain't going to be no ass kicking, man, least of all mine. You're right about one thing, though. You better get out of here."

Benny slid by, "Be careful, be careful."

"Yeah, well I wouldn't give a fuck if he was Al Capone." And Harry took Dali and was heading out when Gino partially blocked them.

"What did I ever do to you, man?"

Harry knocked him down, and looked at the pool of blood and mucous Gino left as he lifted his mouth from the parquet floor. His eyes came up and they looked at Harry's eyes. "And what did I ever do to you, Pussy?"

Three steps closer toward the door, a sudden, rising wail in the room turned Harry around. He saw the two flashes and suddenly remembered that horrible, horrible nightmare he had that time: groped his way, unseeing, to his parents' bed, crawled between them and fell instantly asleep. But his head, slamming against the floor, interrupted the memory. With his last strength, he turned over on his back. He never heard the pistol, or Dali's screaming, although her mouth was but three inches from his face—receding.

DON L. LEE

Black Critic:

The best critics are creative writers, especially published writers who are confident of their worth—which as critics puts them above the common *hatchet men;* Gore Vidal calls them *literary gangsters.* The "frustrated writer" out to build a literary reputation at the expense of others. The competent critic is not a "frustrated writer;" he is a writer who chooses criticism as an extension of his craft. He is also one who goes into criticism with the same honesty and fairness that should be a part of his other creative works.

The black critic is first a blackman, who happens to write; just as the poet, he has the same, if not more, responsibility to his community to perform his function to the best of his ability. He understands the main dilemma of the black writer; "Is he a *writer* who happens to be *black* or is he a *black* man who happens to *write?*" The argument is not a new one. Arna Bontemps speaks of it in connection with some of the post-Harlem Renaissance poets: "But in those days a good many of the group went to the Dark Tower to weep because they felt an injustice in the critics' insistence upon calling them Negro poets instead of just poets. That attitude was particularly displeasing to Countee Cullen." This was the type of illusion that not only would plague the poets but was definitely felt in the other art forms that black people ventured into. As with Countee Cullen, another well-known poet of the post-Harlem Renaissance period, Robert Hayden, refused to acknowledge that he was a "negro" or black poet. Bontemps relates it this way: "One gets the impression that Hayden is bothered by this Negro thing. He would like to be considered simply as a poet." Which is almost like *any* black man in the world saying to the worldrunners that he would like to be considered a man, not a black man. Nonsense! The mere fact that a request of that type is put forth denies the chance of one's being considered anything else. So the point is to stop asking those who can't grant the wish in the first place, and to deal positively with the situation (Addison Gayle calls it the *Black Situation*).

30

Claude McKay, whom Wallace Thurman has referred to as "the only Negro poet who ever wrote revolutionary or protest poetry," was able, like Gwendolyn Brooks, Frank Marshall Davis, Margaret Walker, Melvin B. Tolson, Langston Hughes and Sterling Brown, to deal with the dilemma so that it did not affect his work to the point of *color distortion,* i.e., being one thing and trying to write as another, what Fanon calls black skins, white masks.

We must understand that this will be the decade of the black critic. It will be his responsibility not only to define and clarify, but also to give meaningful direction and guidance to the young, oncoming writers. To perform that function the critic must, if possible, remain detached from his material so that he can fairly filter the music from the noise. So we reiterate that good criticism calls for detachment and fairness, not pseudo-objectivity.

Objectivity at its best is a myth and a very subtle game played on black people. We are a very *subjective* people. All people are. In the final analysis, all one can really try to be is *fair.* One immediately obliterates the whole concept of objectivity when he takes into account the different variables that helped shape our lives. How can one be "objective" about, say, good housing if he has never lived in such; or about hunger if one has been *truly* hungry. How can you be objective about black music if it has played an important part in *your* general survival; or about christianity even though it was forced on you; or about the war if you don't have any power over foreign affairs; or about anything, for that matter, if it involves the human predicament. Objectivity, in matters of importance, such as in the arts, cannot truly exist; true art is as much a part of the culture as is the critic who judges it. So from the get-go the critic is at a disadvantage because he can't disassociate himself fully from that which he is to "objectively" criticize. Some black critics, however, having been schooled in academia, tried to criticize black literature from a different, conventional perspective—and failed. James T. Stewart relates the reason for such failure in this way: "His assumptions were based on white models and on a self-conscious 'objectivity.' This is the plight of the 'negro' man of letters, the intellectual who needs to demonstrate a so-called academic impartiality to the white establishment."

We must understand that white critics write for white people; they are *supposed* to; they owe their allegiance and livelihood to white people. The black critic is in a very precarious position at this time in history; we agree with Albert Murray (and that's unusual) when he said that, "Being black is not enough to make anybody an authority on U.S. Negroes." Being black *is not enough,* but is, at this time, a necessary prerequisite.

It has become increasingly clear that one starts with the roots and then defines the type of tree. That is to say, *any* writer was first black, white, yellow or red before he became a writer. Like the tree, the *to-be-writer* acquired certain characteristics notable in his particular lineage, such as language, religion, diet, education, daily life style. So up to a certain point the *to-be-writer* was just another black, white, yellow or red manchild, right? This is universal: naturally development into manhood is partially pre-determined— which is to say that because of the different cultural patterns of black, white, yellow and red men, there exist normal difference and variety in each of the four mentioned; and each type will look at the world the way he/she has been taught to view it. The core of my argument is that I, as a black man/critic, cannot possibly accurately judge or assess, let's say, Chinese literature. And, if we look at the reasons why un-emotionally, I'm sure you would agree:

> First I can't speak the Chinese language (which means I can't read the literature in the original); second, I never lived among the Chinese people—so I know very little about their daily life style; third, my only knowledge of Chinese religion comes from what I read—which puts me at the disadvantage of accepting someone else's interpretation, which is always dangerous; fourth, my knowledge of Chinese music is terribly limited; fifth, my knowledge of Chinese folklore and dance is negligible; and finally, I've never been to China, so would be unfamiliar with many of the references used in the literature.

Have I made myself clear? The critic is first and foremost a black-man, redman, yellowman, or whiteman who writes. And as a critic, he must stem from the same roots that produced him. How else can his style and content presently be understood? Which brings us to whites who study from the outside looking in, maintaining that they can learn as much about the tree from distant observation as from intimacy, or that they can interpret by anatomically dissecting

32

the organism (keep in mind that even in dissection one has to touch that which one dissects).

With a tree, they may be successful in some of their findings. But in dealing with humans, one has to almost become a part of the humans he wishes to understand. When looking from the outside, one almost has to use the tools of the anthropologist—has to live, sleep, eat, suffer, and laugh among the people about whom one is trying to gain some insight. *No* white critic has done this. Sure, Robert Bone may have had some in-depth conversations with Sterling Brown, but that doesn't give him the tools that are necessary to pass judgment on the entirety of black literature. William Styron may have let James Baldwin spend some time on his farm, but obviously knowing and listening to Baldwin, as perceptive as Baldwin is, doesn't give Styron the sensitivity necessary for recording the adventures of one of our greatest black heroes, Nat Turner. David Littlejohn may have taken a few courses in black literature and sat in on some of the black writers' conferences, but obviously for him all of that was a prerequisite for a bad, pretentious book that Hoyt Fuller rightly maintains should be avoided "like the plague." Edward Margolies lives in the heart of the literary capital; that's where he should stay, and leave the native sons alone. Irving Howe and Richard Gilman had best stay with Jewish and WASP literature respectively, and leave their natural opposites alone; their ignorance is showing in whiteface.

The argument intensifies as the "negro" apologists say the reason Bone, Styron, Littlejohn, Margolies and others tried to write about the black writer is that there were no *black critics* willing to do it. Well, we can look at that statement from two points of view. There have always been black critics, e.g., James Weldon Johnson, William Stanley Braithwaite, Benjamin Griffith Brawley, Sterling A. Brown, Alain Locke, and Nick Aaron Ford, just to mention a few of the earliest. The problem, however, was not that there weren't any competent black critics; the problem was getting into print. Some of our contemporary "black" critics found it not beneficial to make a life out of the study of black literature—still leaving out Africa, the West Indies, and many of the Asian countries. World literature to them meant, naturally, that which was white and western. But there's still time for them to come back; James A. Emanuel pulls their coats when he says that "the pages of *CLA*

Journal, to select but one representative, Negro-managed scholarly publication, are regularly filled with excellent Negro commentary on the works of white authors. If more of such professionally trained Negro critics were to turn their energies to the explication of literature by authors of their race, the enrichment in the feeling and knowledge of both black and white readers would be imponderable."

The black critic—as a black man first and writer second—illustrates a profound understanding of his responsibility to himself and to his community. He is what he reflects or projects. If he moves throughout the world quoting the qualities of John Donne and F. Scott Fitzgerald, that's where he's at; if he marvels at the achievements of William Dean Howells and Francois Rabelais, that's probably where he wants to be, and to try to move him from that point may be an exercise in futility. The black critic like the black creative writer is a part of a people and should not isolate himself into some pseudo-literary wishing land. The black critic/writer must understand that writing is, after all is said and done, a *vocation* like that of a teacher, doctor, historian etc., and becomes a way of life only when established within a concept and identity compatible with the inner workings of the self. That is to say, some of us blacks may *think* we are white, but that concept comes under daily question and contradiction, and is forever inflicting pain on the inner self. We are blackmen who happen to write, not *writers* who happen to be black. If the latter were true, Richard Wright, Ted Joans, William Gardner Smith and Chester Himes would not have left this country; Ralph Ellison would have published another novel by now; Sam Greenlee wouldn't have had to go to England to get his book published; John A. Williams would be as secure and rich as Norman Mailer; *Black World* wouldn't exist; and Frank Yerby, after a long record of denials of his "negroness," wouldn't have published *Speak Now.*

What the black critic must bring to us is an extensive knowledge of world literature, along with a specialized awareness of his own literature. He must understand that a "mature literature has a history behind it," and that that which is being written today is largely indebted to the mature black literature that came before. Thus, if looked at from the proper perspective, the whole of black literature can provide reliable criteria for the new critic to use. The competent black critic will have a love for and an intimate experience with the literature on which he is passing judgment. This will give him a basic philosophy for such judgment. As Stephen Coburn Pepper puts it, "It follows that good criticism is criticism based on a good philosophy. For a good philosophy is simply the best disposition of all evidence available."

We agree with T. S. Eliot in "The Frontiers of Criticism" when he states that "Every generation must provide its own literary criticism, each generation brings to the contemplation of art its own categories of appreciation, makes its own demand upon art, and has its own uses for art." The poet/writer will take the language of others and of his own generation and extend and revitalize it. The poet/writer as critic is at his best when he uses his own poetic talents—for as a poet/writer he is uniquely capable of knowing and understanding the potential of other poet/writers. What the critic does in many cases is make people more aware of what they already feel but can't articulate. The black critic understands that today's poets have revitalized and enriched the language, and in doing so have opened up new avenues of communication among the world's people.

The black critic, like the black poet, must start giving some leadership, some direction. We agree with Darwin T. Turner when he states that, "Despite fifty years of criticism of Afro-American literature, criteria for the criticism have not been established. Consequently, some readers judge literature by Afro-Americans according to its moral value, a few for its aesthetic value, most by its social value, and too many according to their response to the personalities of the Black authors." This narrow-mindedness must end and substantial criteria must come into existence. We can see innovative movement by looking at the statement of purpose of *The Writers' Workshop* of the *Organization of Black American Culture* (OBAC) under the direction of Hoyt Fuller.
That purpose includes the following:

1. The encouragement of the highest quality of literary expression reflecting the black experience.
2. The establishment and definition of the standards by which that creative writing which reflects the black experience it to be judged and evaluated.

3. The encouragement of the growth and development of black critics who are fully qualified to judge and evaluate black literature on its own terms while at the same time cognizant of the traditional values and standards of western literature and fully able to articulate the essential differences between the two literatures.

We're sure that other writers in different parts of the states have traveled or are beginning to travel in similar directions.

We must pull in the brothers and sisters that are academically involved, people like Darwin T. Turner, James A. Emanuel, Addison Gayle, Jr., Richard Long, Catherine Hurst, Stephen Henderson, George Kent, Helen Johnson, Sarah Webster Fabio, W. Edward Farrison, Richard Barksdale and Dudley Randall. We must optimistically encourage the young to continue to see innovative change and standards; let them know that we hear them and are listening to them, because without Carolyn Rodgers, Mary Helen Washington, Johari Amini, David Llorens, Carolyn Gerald, Larry Neal, Toni Cade, Clayton Riley and others, the controversy over criteria and a black aesthetic might not ever have existed.

Lastly, a word of caution to our new and established critics. You cannot be concerned continuously with the intellectual diplomacy such as that of the white critic who before placing his stamp of approval on some studies must first check indexes to see if his name is listed as a reference, thereby perpetuating a closed literary system dangerous for the benefit of black people. For rhetoric can be a dangerous communicative device if it is not correctly used, especially in the world of letters. Black critics who do not have a tradition of social rhetoric must now become masters of an alien language, that is, if black people are to survive. And survival is what we are about. Not individually, but as a people. To quote Addison Gayle, Jr., "The dedication must be to race;" you see, the wolves, ours and theirs, are waiting for us to fail. We have a surprise for them.

Black Writing

We see the Sixties as a movement beyond the shadowiness of the Harlem Renaissance and the restrictiveness of the Negritude Movement. The poets of the Sixties and Seventies move beyond mere rage and "black is beautiful" to bring together a new set of values, emotions, historical perspectives and futuristic direction—a transformation from the lifestyle of the *sayer* to that of the *doer*.

Black writing as we view it today is the result of centuries of slavery and forced alienation from Africa and the self. We've been exiles in a strange land where our whole lifestyle repeatedly faces contradiction after contradiction. Black writing to the African-American is the antithesis of a decadent culture that over the centuries has systematically neglected and dehumanized us with the fury and passion of an unfeeling computer.

Literature produced by black hands is not necessarily black writing. What has to be embodied in blackwriting, first and foremost, is the consciousness that reflects the true black experience, the true African-American experience—related in a style indicative of that experience. Which means that new forms as well as adaptations of forms now in use will have to come into existence. Black consciousness, in any case, can be a conscious or an unconscious effort in blackwriting; if one is black, it's very difficult to write otherwise. We must understand that there will be a pervasive presence of everything and anything that is indigenous to the African-American people.

Black art is a functional art; it is what the Africans call a collective art. It is committed to humanism; it commits the community, not just individuals. As someone has said, black art commits the black man to a future which then becomes present for him, an integral part of himself. The black writer/artist works out of a concrete situation, his geography, his history as well. He uses the materials that are at hand and the everyday things which make up the texture of his life. He rejects the anecdotal, for this does not commit because it is without significance. Black art, like African art, is *perishable*. This too is why it is functional. For example, a black poem is written not to be read and put aside, but to actually become a part of the giver and receiver. It must perform some function: move the emotions, become a part of the dance, or simply make one act. Whereas the work itself is perishable, the *style* and *spirit* of the creation is maintained and is used and reused to produce new works. Here we can see clearly that art for art's sake is something out of a European dream, and does not exist, in most cases, in reference to the black poet.

Most blackart is social: art for *people's* sake. That is, the people will help shape the art, and although the work may not be here forever, through the active participation of the people, its full meaning will be realized. Blackart is total being: it cannot be separated from black life. As Dr. S. Okechukwu Mezu puts it,

> Poetry is . . . a part of human life and does not have to be written and in fact for a long time African poetry was mainly oral and unwritten. In the African village, traveling bards sang songs and recited poetry to the accompaniment of musical instruments. These bards told stories and anecdotes. Some of these recitals were serious and historical, bringing into light the events of war and peace with occasional commentary on the reigns of various chiefs and strong men of the village. Others were lyrical, while a few were coarse and bawdy. But most of them were roundelays and quite often people joined in the narration.

Thus the people reflect the art and the art is the people. This must be understood: the interaction between the writer and his people combined with the interaction between the writer and himself are essential to the aesthetic of blackness. Still, it is impossible to define the black aesthetic. When you try to label or define an area as varied and intricate as the aesthetic of black art, you are bound to be inaccurate. First, by trying conclusively to define and categorize the black aesthetic, you automatically limit it (a specific definition would exclude improvement, advancement and change). You see, no one can really define the white aesthetic—even within the context of traditional western literature; every time a new European-American writer hits the scene, there is an alteration of the white-European aesthetic.

Black writing, as other art forms practiced by black people, is an expression of our attitudes toward the world. The black writer, as the black musician, will continue to define and legitimize his own medium of expression. We agree with the African critic

Mukhtarr Mustapha when he states:

> Afro-American writers and musicians have realized that they are living in a state of crisis, and because a crisis is in most cases short, therefore they cannot afford to expend their energies in verbal excess. . . . This revolutionary state has compelled the writer to search extensively for the most laconic way of stating his case. The writers today in Africa and America are propelled by a desire for condensed expression; the writers' screening time is limited; therefore his task should be leveled towards clarity of thought in short forms: call them poetical tone, movement and shape.

This state of affairs is not a reaction against or a put down of the prose form, but an advancement in the use of the written word in conveying messages and information.

Actually the black writer is a realist and understands that that which hits the hardest leaves the greatest impression—and the hard shot phrasing of a Sonia Sanchez or a Norman Jordan is often more deadly in communicating an idea than the cool, intellectual and subtle prose of a James Baldwin or a John A. Williams. Finally, the black writer/poet is trying to raise the level of consciousness among his people. His message is joy and beauty, pain and hurt, and his ear is close to the dance floor. His work is not "protest," but is a genuine reflection of himself and his people. After all, "protest" writing is generally a poor reaction to somebody or something and often lacks the substance necessary to motivate and move people. There is a profound difference between the quick rhythms of a James Brown and those of a Cecil Taylor—the black writer/poet realizes that and fills the vacuum in between.

Mwilu/ or Poem for the Living
(for Charles and LaTanya)

jump bigness upward
like u jump clean   make everyday the weekend
& work like u party.

u justice brother, in the world of the un
just be there when wanted when needed when
yr woman calls yr name Musyoka* when yr son
wants direction strength give it, suh. suh
we call u strength, suh call u whatever.

be other than the common   build the sky
work:
study the bringers of anti-good,
question Jesus in the real,
& walk knowledge like u walk unowned streets, brother.
read like u eat only betta betta Musomi,*
Musomi be yr name run emptiness into its givers
& collect the rays of wisdom.
there's goodness in yr eyes giver.   give.
yr wind is chicago-big, Kitheka: Afrikan forest right-wind
running   walking dullness of night thinkers in the wrong.

why we rather be evil, momma?
why we ain't togatha, Rev. Cleopolius?
why we slide under hurt with tight smiles of forgiveness, Judas?
why our women want to be men, amana?
why our men want to be something other, Muthusi?
what's goin ta make us   us, Kimanthi?
why we don't control our schools, Mr. Farmer?
why we don't have any land, big negro?
why we against love, pimps?

FRELIMO ** in chicago talkin to the Stones
hear what the real rocks have to say.

**FRELIMO Freedom fighters form Mozambique (south-east Afri-
ca)

be strange in the righteous
move away dumb junkies leaning into death:
   never Muslim eating pig sandwiches never
   never listerine breath even cuss proper never
   never u ignorant because *smart* was yr teacher never
   never wander under wonder fan-like avenues never
   never *will be never* as long as never teaches never.
snatching answers from the blue while
giving lip-service before imitating yr
executors.

jump bigness upward
Impressions putting Fanon to music & sing like
black-rubbermen over smoked garbage cans with
music of a newer year among stolen night in
basement corners meet u in the show, baby
just below the health food sign by sam's with
clean water over oiled fish as mini skirt sisters
wear peace symbols supporting the Isralies as
unfeeling as the *east India company. wdn't dance*
to the words of Garvey on pill hill eating cornbread with a fork in a see-thru walking suit running
the fields of crazy while teaching the whi-te boy
the hand-shake. wd sell yr momma if somebody wd buy her,
hunh. roach-back challenge space after un-eaten spit.
goin ta still call u brother,
goin ta still call u sister too, hunh.

brother, sister.
young lovers of current doo-wops
rake cleanliness brother:
& study un-written words of manhood.
young lovers of current doo-wops
what's yr new name sister:
reflect the goodness of yr man.
like the way u talk to each other, like it.
the way yr voices pull smiles
u $+$ u $= 2$ over 2 which is 1.

raised higher than surprised quietness
kiss each other   and
touch the feel of secret words
while we all walk the
shadows of greatness.

---

* The African names are from the Swahili language of Central &
east Africa.

Mwilu (*Mwi*-lu)	Of black; likes black
Musyoka (Mu-syo-ka)	One who always returns
Musomi (Mu-so-mi)	Scholarly; reads; studies
Kitheka (Ki-*the*-ka)	Wanderer of the forest
Amana (A-ma-na-)	Peacefulness; serenity; feminine
Muthusi (Mu-thu-si)	Pioneer; pathfinder; goes before
Kimanthi (Ki-ma-*nthi*)	One who searches for freedom, wealth, love.

An Afterword: for Gwen Brooks
(the search for the new-song
begins with the old)

knowing her is not knowing her
is not
autograph lines or souvenir signatures & shared smiles
is not
pulitzers, poet laureates or honorary degrees,
you see   we ordinary people
just know
ordinary people.

to read gwen is to be,
to experience her in the *real*
is the same,   she is her words.   more
like a fixed part of the world   is there
quietly penetrating   slow
reminds us of a willie kgositsile love poem   or
isaac hayes singing *one woman.*

still
she suggests more;

have u ever seen her home?
it's an idea of her: a brown wooden frame
trimmed in dark gray with a new screen door.
inside: looks like the lady owes everybody on the southside
        nothing but books momma's books.
her home like her person is under-fed and small.

gwen:
pours smiles of african-rain
a pleasure well received among uncollected garbage cans
and heatless basement apartments.
her voice the needle for new-songs
plays unsolicited messages: poets, we've all seen
poets. minor poets ruined by
minor fame.

With All Deliberate Speed
(for the children of our world)

in july of 19 somethin
the year of the "love it or leave it" stickers,
a pink sharecropper former KKK   now
a wallace pro-bircher
undercover minuteman
living in N.Y. city   as
a used hardhat flag waving,
beer belly torn undershirt wearen
hawk.

is also
an unread bible carrying preacher
& secret draft dodger from WW 2
who
went to washington d-c.
at government's expense   for
the 1970 honor america day   and
support our boys in viet nam

also
took time out to find
& wildly   slap   slap   slap   slap
one
B.A., M.A., LLD., N.E.G.R.O.,
supreme court justice in the mouth   and
with all deliberate speed
went home to alabama
to brag about
it.

To Be Quicker
For Black Political Prisoners/ on the Inside
and Outside —— *Real*
(To My Brothers and Sisters of OBAC)

clamb ape mountain backwards
better than the better u thought u had to be better than
jump clean, cleaner.
jump past lighting into field-motion, feel-motion, feel mo
feel mo than the world thought u capable of feelin.
cd do it even fool yr momma, jim! fool yrself, hunh—

goin ta be cleaner,   hunh.
goin ta be stronger,   hunh.
goin ta be wiser,   hunh.
goin to be quick to be quicker   to *be*

quick to be whats needed to be whats needed:
quicker than enemies of the livingworld,
quicker than cheap smiles of a cadillac salesman,
quicker than a dead junky talking to the wind,
quicker than super-slick niggers sliding in the opposite,
quicker than whi-te-titty-new-left-what's-left suckin niggers,
quicker to be quick, to be quick.

u wise brother,
u wiser than my father was when he
talked the talk he wasn't suppose to talk.

quicker to be quick, to be:

a black-African-fist slapping a wop-dope pusher's momma,
a hospital a school anything workin to save us to pull us
closer to Tanzania to Guinea to Harlem to the West Indies to
closer to momma to sister to brother closer to closer to
FRELIMO to Rastafory to us to power to running run to build
to controllifelines to Ashanti to music to life to Allah closer
to Kenya to the black world to the rays of anti-evil.

clamb ape mountain backwards brother
feel better than the better u thought was better
its yr walk brother,
lean a little, cut the smell of nasty.
jump forward into the past
to bring back

goodness.

Positives for Sterling Plumpp

can u walk away from ugly,
will u sample the visions of yr self,
is ugly u?   it ain't yr momma, yr woman,
            the brother who stepped on yr alligator shoes,
            yr wig wearen believing in Jesus grandmomma, or
            the honda ridden see-thru jump suit wearen brother.

yeah,
caught u upsidedown jay-walking across europe
to catch badness running against yr self.
didn't u know u were lost brother?
confused hair with blackness
thought u knew it before the knower did,
didn't u know u lost brother?
thought u were bad until u ran up against BAD:
Du Pont, Ford, General Motors even the latest

45

Paris fashions: & u goin ta get rich off dashikis before sears.
didn't u know u were lost brother?

beat laziness back into the outside,
run the mirror of ugliness into its inventors,
will u sample the visions of yr self?
quiet   like the way u do it soft spoken   quiet
quiet   more dangerous than danger a new   quiet
quiet   no name quiet no number quiet pure   quiet
quiet   to pure to purer.

a full-back clean-up man   a black earthmover
my main man
change yr name like the wind
blow in any direction catch righteousness,
u may have ta smile at the big preacher in town,
thats alright organize in the church washrooms,
trick the brother into learning—
be as together as a 360 computer:
          can u think as well as u talk,
          can u read as well as u drink,
          can u teach as well as u dress?
sample the new visions of yr work brother   & smile
we'll push DuBois like they push the racing form.

yr woman goin ta look up to u,
yr children goin ta call u hero,
u my main nigger
the somethin like the somethin
u ain't suppose   *to be.*

WALTER BRADFORD

Sketches of a Trip Home

Depending on where you are and the conditions, eighteen days can be a long, unimaginative strain or a revival. For me eighteen days in Africa was a revival, a return to consciousness, an ancient human consciousness. I could feel myself absorbing, taking in, through pores I never knew I had, or had forgotten how to use.

Africa told me about me and my people and anticipated the hunger of her children in exile. She is warm, she is color, she is a song, a long lyrical song.

Chicago had been the beginning for me, like how I got born, good hot lovin' and several years between airflights.

But that matter didn't matter once the plane was up and gone, and sixteen minutes out of Dayton, I knew I had left home. Up now beside the Sun, visions of a lonesome niggah danced on the flying wing that shook from Mecca's ancient wind and said to me, "C'mon home, son, C'mon home." Now the carrier arrogantly pushed through clouds that swirled around it like thickly painted music. The silence was massive. The plane that had looked huge and capable on the ground quivered obediently as it intruded on the scene above the clouds. I sat like the rest, in straight row chairs hoping we wouldn't have to make the ultimate comparison. Everybody talked to forget the streaks of black that yielded more of the same. I felt safe.

You can never see the earth catch up with the Sun. Instead, small lights sparkle on edges so far away they make you dream as you watch them. Then the Sun, in grand announcement, places itself in front of you. It's a fresh day, a never-breathed-on day, a never touched or abused day, a new day all your own.

And then I saw her; Africa stood up and rolled back the green so I could see the holes in her breast and the scars that lay like lengths of rope pasted over the wounds of her body. And Cairo smiled and glinted her gift of picture-gold sand, Nommo soared a burning funnel to welcome me and Judah spoke as the Sun halo-ed his form; "No need to stand at the gate trembling to come in, trembling for what to say. Be at peace in this heaven for it is your home."

> Africa roars
> she causes loins
> Africa gives greenness
> ah home,
> Africa raps
> through wind tubes (she told me in a song)
> Africa sighs like woman
> Africa is where I belong.

First day in Cairo. What perfect syncopation yields the land, the people, the air; and the Sun plays bass harmony to it all. I stalk the land (I have the wrong pace) clumsy like a wild thing with no sense of quiet, no sense, no sense at all.

> But the wholeness of her body, the completeness
> of her mind, made me walk the walk of history
> with eternal Egypt on my mind.

The Bazaar is us. The bazaar is 47th street, hustlers of a grand tradition. And the money changers are in the temples; now they flow into the street, into the hallways and alleys and across the passage to a land called promise, deafricanized.

East now to the pyramids. I pass green gardens and hear prayers of light; barefoot boys and timeless men pace the Nile to the golden triangles. It is a plot to get you to feeling the way they feel.

And when I see the pyramids I want to pray. I want to scream "Allah, I have found you" and sit in the ancient seat of sand and be an ancient mood, be a calmness, be a calmness that endures. be.

Now the Emperor's land is a grand land where gentleness is the strongest force. The people notice you and say love. "Hello. You Afro-American?" I say yes. "Welcome to my shop . . . this is my brother, my cousin and my nephew," he says, his English straining through Amharic. I talk and feel good inside. They listen and ask for my words. I dance the dance kings had danced, and I hear the choir of coptic lions that put us to sleep. Now the day hours are cool even while the Sun is awake—winter time they say, rains once in the morning, Sun shines after then and once in the evening just as night begins . . . and the stars they be angry,

angry in they skin, they so bright they have to shine one at a time they give off so much light.

There is music. National music. National black music. Black men with accents for brows, and women orderly on their own, have good cause to sing even when I said good-bye.

In Tanzania there is gold, in Tanzania there is gold, in Tanzania there is gold and there are diamonds and streams of yellow honey that run from the trunks of trees, flowers in purple and orange and green and greener greens sucked upward by the Sun. The people are colors. Colors on the inside that burst through and share laughter with you, share the fundamentals. The sea is at the front door, the forest is at the back, I take my choice of histories and I know the color of black.

And we ride along the coast, I see much of what I don't understand but it's ended and the song is clear when we stop at the MOJO FILLING STATION. And Tanzania wraps her air around you like a woman who's missed her man too long and invents his shoulders to kiss and the bone in his neck to put her lips on.

I felt what she gave and responded slowly at first, for how do you love a queen? Then with all the energy I could create and the control to make the goodness last, I pressed my body against hers and slid my hands softly across each part of her I could reach. She dazzles me. Now I bury my face in the span between her breast and arm—it's as long as the coast—and wait for morning to repeat, with improved grace, the dream that dances in front of me. I love you, Heaven of Peace. And she blinks and tells me to return.

A Blk Social Statement
on the Occasion of
Another Curtis Ellis Creation

Anything creative is preceded by a need; like ah baby, ah building, th Sunshine, ah pome.

A creation is a prideful, arrogant revival of everything original, everything pure.

A creation is a willingness to continue, to endure despite the routine harshness.

We blk people need the pride of having done something completely our own. We need the feel of accomplishment, the element on which history gets built and generations improve on and give thanks to hip fore-parents for answering all the basics, giving us time to explore and prepare the next level.

In addition, we need the one stick that makes creation worthwhile; collective responsibility. Each of us needs to be responsible to the whole of us, down to the smallest lost blk pebble. If that pebble be a dopey sittin' on 16th and Homan noddin' we must accept the nodding stupor and what it implies for us collectively or eliminate him altogether as a block to change or make him as functionally valuable as possible. Our expectation should be no greater than the substance it comes from. Creation is a giver of direction.

For the dough we spend on dope, suede kadillacs, college educations, operas, baseball games, we can baptize our minds (where change begins) with the realness that sits on shelves, waiting for us to quit chasing ourselves whirlpool style, and return to the ancient goodness from which we all come.

Do ya' hear that . . . do ya hear that phrase he sang from his goodness, "Everybody can be great cause everybody can serve" . . . do u hear that, do ya' hear that those whose self hate and crusty guilt about it causes them to kill the ugliness in other blks, praying it will erase their own . . . do u hear that Blk p. stone, disciples, vice lords, cobras, panthers, us, any lonesome niggah lookin' for something to love . . . do u hear, do ya' hear record makin' syl Johnson, record makin' syl Johnson singin' to the sisters; 'Don't give it ahway, don't give that thang ahway' which implies mass but sophisticated prostitution. He should ask he mamma if he daddy made that intellectual proposition befo' he come on the scene . . . do u hear, do ya' hear that Phds, hpds, or is it ams or pms wid the attache'/purse full of fried chickin' lookin' for ah home, america sho ain't yoos, mine or the brother or sister u claim u cant communicate wid cause they speech patterns be undeveloped, do u hear that, do u hear that? . . . but did u see him, did u see our tel-le-vision niggah, our crosseyed tel-le-vision niggah, our cross-eyed tel-le-vision niggah wid th processed toupe' who straddle a mule backwards and thought he was on the flight of the golden angus . . . or did u see th contrast, did u see the boy/man who came down from the mountain to say something creative, said I am a revoluushun-ary ah big head niggha standin' at th edge of th world wid his dick in his hand talkin' bout I am a revoluushun-ary?

No matter no matter the confusion and the contradictions now, for the essence of it all is to narrow our contradictions to the point we can control and finally diminish them. And when tha's done we should say thanks the way a newly ordained 47th street hustler said "All praises be to al-lahh, my man." Peace.

The Confessions
of Nat Turner

The new emphasis on a national black literature makes white values no longer useful in judging the literary perspective of blacks.
A review by a black man;
WALTER BRADFORD

The title of the book, The Confessions of Nat Turner, by William Styron, white writer, is incorrect; it should be, "The Resurrection of Nat Turner." For it was Styron's aim to use the writer's expansive imagination to dramatize his sensitivity to the soul who presumably confessed to the crimes he was hanged for, then it missed the center of target and landed somewhere near the craggy edges of white objectivity.

Styron's Turner was a "remarkable negro preacher" who led the only "effective sustained revolt in the annals of negro slavery." He was born the property of Benjamin Turner in Southampton, County, Virginia in 1800, and through his mother's inheritance of house niggah status from her mother, who died at thirteen from childbirth and insanity, Nat was third generation beneficiary of the position.

He learned to read first by struggling with the labels on jars and canisters in the pantry of the big kitchen where he worked.

Later, he graduated to stealing the bible and other books from the gothic library of the master's house. One day he was caught hiding in the pantry reading a copy of his booty by the head house niggah, little Morning, who promptly turned him over to Marse Turner for punishment. Marse Turner was kind, the writer says, and instead of scolding Nat, he encouraged him. He even had his wife and daughter help the little kitchen slave learn his alphabet. Considering the general condition of slaves, Styron continues, Nat was well off. But he didn't know or appreciate it until the turning point of the story when the author allowed Nat's emotions to catch up with the events in his life.

When Marse Turner had to sell all the slaves because of the high price of keeping a plantation, he saved Nat for last, promising that his new master would surely see to it that Nat finished his carpentry trade, got some schooling and finally purchased his own freedom.

But it didn't happen that way; Nat's new master was a homosexual capitalist preacher who kept the profits from Nat's work as a hired laborer, then sold him to slave brokers for a generous capital gain.

It was not until he was in the niggah pin, the author insists, that Nat realized he really was a slave and subject to the same treatment as his fellow pin dwellers. More significantly, he realized Marse Turner had lied to him. Thereafter, he made no distinctions. He distrusted and hated all whites.

Nat had continued to read the bible and by the time he was sold to his last owner Travis, he knew he had been "ordained for some great purpose." On August 21, 1831, that "great purpose" began. When it ended some twenty miles and three days later, fifty-seven white men, women and children were dead. Three months later Nat Turner was hanged and his body turned over to doctors " . . . who skinned it and made grease of the flesh. Mr. R. S. Barham's father owned a money purse of his hide . . . his skeleton was for many years in the possession of Dr. Massenberg, but has since been misplaced."

Styron's account of Nat Turner makes some desperate assumptions about black life, particularly black slave life. He assumes, despite his whiteness, to know the mind, soul, body and heart of a black man.

Outrageous. Can't be done.

But it isn't enough to say he can't do it merely because he's white; it's much deeper than that. The sensibilities are inextricably different. The chants, feelings, tastes and sounds of any black world are not the same, organically, as those of a white world.

Example: the senses that are nourished by red beans and rice and hot water corn bread are more likely to manifest themselves in the african Boo-ga-loo than the Irish jig. Here is the assumption that he can create and be a black man (and it's only one of the neurotic revelations of this novel);

> Rank intuition . . . if you can sympathize with the dispossessed, you can certainly take on the lineaments of the negro. To assume that one can't would raise a most dangerous point, such as, to deny Jimmy Baldwin's right to write from the view of white people, as he has done, or to suggest that the races are so far apart that even "Othello" cannot be considered valid art.

I submit that "rank intuition" has to take on the lineaments of the facts, which means seeing a slave's life as he would record it or through the senses of his still chained ancestors, before any sympathizing can be done. Sympathizing is always a lesser emotion than the realness and immediacy to the person experiencing the event. The "dispossessed" he mentioned wasn't a reference to the novel nor was it the universal European serf.

On the contrary, he was an african who had a land and culture that included the same incidentals that comprised the cave dwellers' culture; language; art, government, religion, love, hate . . .

But blacks received slave treatment by profitable design from the time they arrived here until they were hanged, sold or emancipated away.

Styron uses James Baldwin to assist him in his tedious distortions Baldwin says of the novel: "He has begun with a common history, ours." I think he means black American history or white American history or maybe American history, I am not sure. Perhaps Baldwin isn't either. More insulting is how Styron expects us to believe that a white can step into a black soul the same way he masquerades on Halloween. He forgets that our imitation of whites comes from the inside down under position where we saw (and are still seeing) the dreadful introverted impotence of night transferred to pulpits and how our mothers and grandmothers raised white children and listened while white parents spoke of our parents as if they, and the rest of us, were invisible.

But finally, speculation on whether the races are "far apart" is boring. So is considering *Othello* as "valid art." First, Shakespeare was white, and we have been saturated with the goodness and sanctity of Willie Shakespeare. Second, he never had the opportunity to reflect on the euphuism "Black is beautiful, baby" as related to the style and focus of LeRoi Jones, Ed Bullins and Ron Milner.

None of this matters anyway, Othello and Nat were in the end examples of "valid art"; two dead niggahs.

The Virginia born writer assigns Nat an incredible tolerance level of emotional stress. He lets the boy Nat witness his mother copulating with an Irish driver man on the kitchen table of the big house, between sweeping and scrubbing the floors. Nat's reaction is; "I thought it (screwing) was an obsession, or something of niggahs alone."

But Marse Styron doesn't stop there; he has Nat keep the faith through the faggot preacher until he is in the niggah pin where then and only then does it begin to appear to him that maybe white folks don't love him. It's unbelievable that a slave could not, at a very early age, determine that he was a slave and create a method of survival.

For Styron to admit that men, not slaves, survived the system and grew to hate whites would be a contradiction of the Puritan Ethic he protects by writing this book. For instance, it doesn't bother him to write about the homosexual preacher, a clear projection of his insight into his environment, which is what any writer writes from, and at the same time allow his bible to be used as a revolutionary's handbook. To admit that one contradiction, that every commandment from the bible is suppositional, he has to admit that his (and ultimately their) morals are as transitory as the "girl with golden curls" Nat envisioned whenever Styron had him masturbating in the woodshed.

These tenets clash and sparkle very clearly when they are set beside Nat's purely moral, political and revolutionary acts which were to kill all the whites between Southampton County and the swamp some twenty miles away, establish a camp there, as many blacks had been and were doing and live out his life hoping his acts would inspire other blacks to move for their own freedom in the same fashion.

No slave masters, no slaves. Direct and revolutionary.

Instead of subsiding, the contradictions become lies. Styron made Nat an indecisive revolutionary lacking the courage to kill, lacking the power to control his men, lacking belief in himself.

Herbert Aptheker, William Lloyd Garrison and Southern historian W. S. Drewy refute these concepts categorically. And Nat, in his confessions, says; "I was not addicted to stealing in my youth, nor have ever been—yet such was the confidence of the negroes in my neighborhood in my superior judgment, they would often carry me with them when they were going on any roguery . . . having soon discovered (that) to be great I must appear so, and therefore studiously avoided mixing in the society and wrapped myself in mystery, devoting my time to fasting and prayer." According to that, Nat understood himself and his people very well.

His *confessions,* however, are at least suspect. Their information must be weighed and measured from the values pertinent to a black world. Because when you consider the *Confessions* were recorded by a white Southern lawyer, who was acting as any human would, to protect and enhance his cultural and political position, and that slave owners had been, long before Turner's revolt, nearly psychotic with fear of slave uprisings, you begin to understand the nature of white objectivity, the essence of which was profit and the moral contradictions. Remember, that over one hundred blacks were killed in Southampton alone after Nat's impudent attempt to change the status quo.

Further, Styron tries to make us believe that blacks help put down the revolt " . . . and to believe it" writes Aptheker, "or offer it (as evidence) shows an utter misapprehension of the nature of slavery."

Nat refers to his father, mother and grandmother in the *Confessions*. His father and mother taught him to read and his grandmother encouraged his bible reading. Styron doesn't mention or infer that these events took place or could have happened. White objectivity!

But his "meditation on history" as he refers to the book, is successful largely because the vehicle, the writing, has a substantial portion of convincing craftsmanship. Ironically, the best written parts are the descriptions of the blacks killing the whites.

> and it was at that instant that Travis' head, gushing blood from a matrix of pulpy crimson flesh, rolled from his neck and fell to the floor with a single bounce, then lay still. The headless night shirted body slid down the wall with a faint hissing sound and collapsed in a pile of skinny shanks, elbows, knobby knees. Blood deluged the room in a foaming sacrament.

And Nat watches one of his men perform a political act:

> Once again the act was done with prodigious speed and intensity; again in its absolute devotion and urgency it was as if by his embrace this scarred tortured little black man was consummating at last, ten thousand old swollen moments of frantic unappeasable desire . . . his downward seeking head mashed her face and mostly hid it all but for the tangled tresses of her hair and the pupil of one eye, wildly quivering, which cast me a glint of lunatic blankness even as the hatchet made a final chunk-chunk and became still.

Two of his earlier novels *Lie Down in Darkness* and *Set This House on Fire* stand out for their well written violence.

The responses Styron received from blacks, specifically black writers, has astonished him. They did not accept his surrealistic church sermon. They did not because they reject the inadequate historical background that made it possible for Styron to write the book.

The white reviewers, along with their negro chattels desperately defended the history and the objectivity of whites. Phillip Rahv in New *York Review of Books* sums it up; "I think that only a white Southern writer could have brought if off . . . a Negro writer, because of a very complex anxiety . . . would have probably stacked the cards, producing in a mood of unnerving rage and indignation a melodrama of saints and sinners."

That's a white man talking about protecting his sanity in the way his history has taught him. Negroes can't write about themselves lest they become "unnerving" or, lest they "stack the cards." He doesn't mention how Styron "stacked the cards" by not telling the truth about Turner's life. For example, Nat had a wife who lived as a slave on another plantation. Could a black writer have treated that bit of information better than a white Southern writer? Could a black writer have been "unnerving" in describing and exploding the sickness and the sicker myths that whites conjure about blacks; could a black writer have answered more accurately the necessity of Nat's actions based on his own experiences than a white Southern writer?

History seems to be repeating itself but this time the judges and recorders are different. Whites will no longer influence let alone determine what black values should be. If they should insist, they should prepare for what this century's prophet has said; "God gave Noah the rainbow sign, no more water, children, the fire next time."

RONDA DAVIS

Invitation
(To the Night and All Other Things Dark)

dark, black robe
one day at night
i will crack
into u
will i crack?

tell me
will u be an endless blackboard
starry chalk screeching against u
until i scream: stop it stop it
and
am found limp by some fool
who won't understand
what i need
to stand?

tell me
will u bust my head
like some dime store alarm
drumming unpluggable falsetto
                    after falsetto
                    after falsetto
until i bleed
into u?

who is out there with u, dark?
a puzzle part that needs me
or
a faceless man who stalks
and dares me to look
and let go
of the light
for the introduction i fear?

perhaps i won't come.
but,
u pull me to coming.
do u suppose
that
in coming
i will come?
will what is in my tangled head
tremble downward, trickle outward
when u save me
from myself?

Poems about Playmates

I.   Sampson

we didn't think
nuthin
of stalkin silver death
on that
el track
playground
daring that third rail
to do something
(it wasn't never turned on nohow)
till
that time
when
yellow Sampson
proved his strength
and
roasted black
glued erect
like a
totem pole
that
his momma

almost
didn't recognize—
we was little biddy cats
but
i can still smell him
in my dreams.

II.   Bubbles

Bubbles
was
too much man
to say he hurt
when
he fell on that nail.
shoooot!
he could take a scratch.
and when it
took his leg
that fall
had
slipped
from his mind.
he was too busy
haulin pop bottles
an
carrying groceries
on Saturday mornings.

spacin

sometimes
i cool out
on this world

i be spacin
tunin in
on clouds

communin
with air

but
dam!
that ain't so
es. o. ter. ic

anybody
can
get hi

Parasitosis

parasitosis
is a white disease
like,
i mean,
lice
ain't never been no problem of ours

parasitosis
grows fat
on soul hosts
drinks black blood
and
vomits HEPsomania
    —which is to say—
ain't got no cool 'bout itself
when it eats something live
other than
pig
and cow

parasitosis
crawls in black back doors
to get pinched
and pronounced real
lest it remain

a dead bug
or
some other blood-thirsty dried-up menace

thinks funk can be translated
into
something
white
and still be funk

beeps bop talk
like a car—muh-kan-ni-kul—like reeull cooull meeun.

parasitosis
is paralytic
from the lice down
but
—if nourished—
will allow a twist—non-African, that is
if u start it off
count for it
and move its arms
out of its way.

parasitosis
got a itch
it cain't scratch
been operating on nubs since it first called us niggahs.

A Personality Sketch: Bill

Bill
exists.
never lives
like the rose
that wilts
only after it dies.

Planted
in the business world,
a yes man.
Noncommittal.

Supervisor,
supervised by fears.

Afraid
of the tremor
in his voice.

The office trivia,
a weed.

The Button Pusher
whose morning task—the hardest—
is slapping on that smile.

Who breathes deep upon arrival
and departure. Respiration.

Whose daily peak
(he grows in the dark)
is the silent solace
of the men's room.

Bill.
The blood of democracy,
but always the
loser.

A living compromise
aiming to please.

Super-Soul Successfully Salaried.
Enviable, but unenvied,
he commands tears,
which,
like the rain,
may bring him life
or
drown his misery.

LINYATTA
(Doris Turner)

3 Units Single Cycle (or)
"Now We Can Be Friends..."

Francina stood before the mirror, embarked upon five minutes of merciless inspection. Still, after she saw that the tailored white skirt and vest hung straight and that the crepe blouse did not escape the skirtband—still, after giving a final shake to the smoothly brushed hair, and a thoughtful tap upon the white and gold linoleum with a sleekly-shod foot, she remained standing detached and aloof, even from herself. Sunlight filtered through pale pink curtains beyond her bed, glimmering idly against sloping walls, white wood of chair and dressing table, the soft fur of numerous stuffed toys. Against this glow, radio blared the remaining 45 seconds of Jimmy Smith's "Organ-Grinder Swing," half-masking "goddammits," "bastards," and "black bitches" (sounds-verbal) irregularly erupting from below.

Suddenly, mechanically, she snapped her fingers, nodded approval to her mirrored image, turned on her heel. Reminded herself that she'd swallowed her vitamins, set her radio for automatic turn-off, and re-reminded herself to check the appointment book regarding the evening engagement—Tony or Lester? . . . Yik yuk blah.

Francina selected a fashion magazine to read during the 40-minute ride to the Loop, picked up her pocketbook and keys and left the room. At each gravitational tug toward the nether region, the voices issued plainer.

"You're such an asinine nigger! No one could've ever told me I'd marry such an asinine nigger!" Laura Kerry was fuming as Francina reached the bottom stair.

"Oh shut the hell up!" returned Joseph Kerry. "Why don't you shut the hell up? If you think your ritualistic morning profanity is going to change me, you're a bigger damn fool than I thought."

"Someday, after all these twenty years, you filthy sonofabitch, you'll learn to quit telling me to shut up! I wish to goddam hell that you'd get your ass out and go see your goddam black bitchy whore so I'll have some peace in this house today!"

"'Black bitchy whore,' huh? I'll bet if those people next door call the damn cops for you disturbin' the peace and slanderin' that wife again, you'll shut your simple mouth for awhile. Takin' you off to the nuthouse where you belong'll fix *you*, woman.

"Take you, you lying sonofabitch, along with that whorecult you're givin' money to . . . "

Blandly, Francina's mind reflected on the scene's semi-reality. It didn't even sound like the woman saying "You jive Maryland farmer" on LOU RAWLS LIVE. It was obvious that if she could have left another way, she would have, and as she rounded the corner, Joseph Kerry demanded: "Good morning!"

Disgust edging her blandness, Francina answered automatically "Um-hm. Good morning."

"Good morning," said Laura Kerry also, and "Have you taken your pills?"

"Yes, Mother. Good morning and goodbye."

"Have a nice day," said Laura Kerry as Francina left the two of them to their morning calisthenics. And wondered vaguely at her mother's insistence on adding "black" to "bitches" to emphasize "bitchiness."

On her way out, Francina glanced into Roberta's room; it was littered with 4 to 6 unhangered miniskirts and dresses, seldom-shined shoes, half-matched plastic jewelry. Sprinkled about were replicas of Roberta's night out—50c-brand wine bottles, purloined *True Confession* magazines, and numerous plaid caps slightly rimmed with Duke's, Murray's or a LaTee's "special." Sprawled somewhere under the bedspread and some sweaters was Roberta. Francina exhaled a small sigh of relief and half-shook her head against the hyper-criticality and faint vinegar odor descending upon her DuBarry-powdered nose. As she turned from the door, hoping that Roberta would wake and go to dancing class, dance far away from plaid caps and long-playing low-paying so-called raps, meprobamate memories flashed her mind-margin, sliding turkey-cold chill between her shoulder blades . . . Out of four human bodies under the same roof for almost two decades, there was not one strong enough for another's salvation . . .

. . . Facing her exit was the row of new living-room curtains, tied in knots by Laura Kerry allegedly to keep Joseph from signaling with them to members of his cult—had Francina walked into the bathroom, she would have seen that Joseph had again refrained both from washing out his bathtub and having the drain fixed so that the water would run out in less than a half-hour . . .

. . . As in faithful recitation, Francina's mind flash-mimeoed the stepfather her best friend Margo three years ago had had for one year, had thrown her mother downstairs, the night she and Josine had fled Josine's back door ducking bottles . . . She stopped more in front of a mirror to check possible hanging-slip signs.

Morning was a soon-to-be-hot warm, and for that Francina could wait. The bus came after five minutes, the "L" train less than that. Francina thought: "Too, too smooth. Much too smooth. Point #1 is: I wonder what's going to happen when I stop lying to myself? #2: I'm not going to stop because states of phobia impair my functioning ability AND Point #3: If I stop, won't anyone else, so I'll be right back where I started from *anyway*."

She looked around. The train had an average crowd. Many of the passengers, like Francina, wore tinted glasses, less to protect their eyes from the sun than the gaze of others.

"Who said," mused Francina, "that one's soul is mirrored in one's eyes? If I thought I saw a soul, I wouldn't trust what I thought I saw."

At Cermak Road, a group of rough-looking white boys crowded through the open doors; behind them crept an elderly, neat black lady, wearing a very clean, very faded cotton print dress and an old straw hat, and an expression of genteel contempt. She carried an armful of old boxes, one of which fell from her arms to Francina's feet. Francina retrieved the package and offered her a seat.

"Thank you and God bless you," the lady said.

Francine smiled and said, "You're welcome."

One of the white boys snickered.

Francina paid them no attention.

"My, you're dressed pretty," the elderly lady said. "And bless you, you have such nice manners. You know, young people nowadays ain't got politeness the first. It's so nice to meet one what's parents taught them somethin'."

Francina relayed her appreciation and agreement.

"At least," continued the lady, "you can be polite to your own kind—it's a shame to see colored people who forget how, don't you agree?"

Francina said, "Yes ma'am, although I don't believe color should be a decisive factor where one's manners are concerned."

"God's truth it is, honey! Bless you, just bless you!"

Francina thought that if she was blessed too much more, her seat in a place she didn't quite believe in would nevertheless be assured. However, the train was approaching Washington St., so she said polite goodbye to the lady and escaped, her spool-sized, elegant heels clicking staccato against the pavement, up subway stairs and into the depth of the lake-bordered, concrete-sealed metropolis.

Her receptionist job in Monsieur Jean's beauty salon was the best summer job she'd had ever, probably the best she would ever have unless Monsieur hired her again for the final summer.

Monsieur Jean was born Haitian, but raised in New Orleans. He was coffee-colored, slender, thirty-eight and fashionable. His customers were white, yellow, and black, and his prices exorbitant as his coiffures were lavish. His two chief assistants were both male, both younger than he, both attractive, both unmarried. Monsieur Jean was married, but his wife was never seen in the vicinity of his salon, and it was whispered that Monsieur enjoyed his *affairs* with men as well as women. Sometimes Monsieur took Francina to lunch, but was never less than polite, considerate and of course utterly charming.

Francina sometimes brought her own lunch in a Bahamian-carved basket engraved with shining peaches and crescents and which resisted rain like coconut shell. She had purchased it upon something called *impulse* and it sometimes caused considerable eyebrow raising. But on this Friday, after a morning of telephone-answering, customer-greeting, appointment-checking, Francina paused, rested her chin against carefully-lacquered fingernail-tips and played mental eeny-meeny-miny & mo with Don Roth's, Stouffers, and the South Pacific.

Exactly at 11:35, Francina was on the street, directed towards the South Pacific which she had deliberately, yet with forced indifference, avoided for no less than a year. At the corner of State

Street, she suddenly hesitated, half-colliding with someone behind her.

"Ohh!" she said aloud and without much expression, "Excuse me . . . "

"Francina!"

She thought: "Uh-huh. I knew morning was too smooth for true."

"Francina!"

She considered: "Remarkable how I thought I understood before and understand better now." Clear and precise as ticker-tape.

Remoteness returned. Francina said, "Why, hello Karl."

" 'Hello,' yourself. This must be one of your low energy-level days. Let's get out of this traffic. Going to lunch?"

"Yes . . . "

"Me, too. South Pacific?"

She thought: Yeah, smart-ass. You would. Wouldn't anyone else have said *that*.

Emotional distance doubled, nevertheless, she heard herself stutter, mentally pinched herself for discipline.

Always he had walked with longer steps than hers could be, and that had not changed.

"You look *very* well, my dear.

"I know," she said. "I get paid for looking *very* well." It slipped out before she thought, but she heard pure amusement in his laughter. It wasn't total conceit on her part, just a requirement of Monsieur Jean's.

Francina suddenly looked up at the sky, wondered at its queer picture-brightness above the stone of tall buildings. Sun glow directed her to smile, and for the first time there was a light in her face as she looked up at the tall man beside her—its undisguised radiance shocked him.

Yet, she knew it all to be false.

Down a curving stair they went, two slender cardboard-figures, accomplished, courteous, resolute. Francina wondered why she had expected the South Pacific would have changed. In any way that mattered, it hadn't. A crisp, black-haired waiter of middle-age, wearing the standard Hawaiian-print shirt, efficiently seated them in the shadow of a palmed ledge. In the table's center a blue-glassed candle

68

threw half-mocking light upon their proper prelude of trivial chit-chat.

She knew Karl's poise as native, not chosen.

She, outwardly serene, felt the dualism of her gilded brightness pressing hard upon her temples. Karl ordered egg-foo-yung, she silently, sharply, remembering how much he liked it.

Karl watched her order chicken-salad and gin-and-tonic. To the drink he would have once objected verbally. Now they both knew he no longer had the right. He had known upon her first smile that he would be allowed no retributions should she choose to tell half-truths.

Through the meal Francina chattered, brittle-bright in wit and laughter. She could not dispel the foreign radiance, yet darkness continued to gnaw its edges. Still, coiled within control of self she curdled, confident.

Finally, abruptly, he said: "I had to leave you, Francina." And looked hard at her, as if to read reaction in her eyes. She chose not to return his gaze, felt her self withdraw automatically, yet painfully, far into herself, into shadow. Still the serenity-pretense, knowing he was at least half-tricked.

"Of course, Karl. It was over. It had been over for quite a few months."

Shock. He had half-expected this, but not with the brain-banging force of polite remoteness.

He had nothing to say for a matter of moments. He and she sat, cardboard and silent in blue shadow and powder-gold candle-light. In all its dusky irony, that blue shadow glowed beneath arrogantly downcast lashes, sparkled electrically against the jewel-blue of Francina's ring. And the long fingers rested thin, controlled, tense, in the fraudulent brightness.

"You still wear the ring," Karl said.

"But yes. A beautiful ring, looking well on my hand. You did give me very lovely presents, Karl—they are for wearing."

Lovely presents for wearing. Simple as that. Final as 11:59 before 12:00.

He said, "It was a long letter that you wrote. I knew that you would do something, but I didn't know exactly what. You always did surprise one, Francina."

Francina's small shoulder-shrug seemed a thing from a trance, and she lit a cigarette over the candle flame. "C'est la vie."

"Almost exactly," he said, "the tone of the letter."

"There is nothing to discuss about the letter."

Then she did look up into his eyes, through the candle-blue haze. She felt that her face was a plaster-paris mask, boated in puppet-painter's enamel, with two holes for eyes, and an irreparable gash for a mouth. Whoever or whatever she was had withdrawn completely, so that only a shell glimmered above the stark light. Whatever he said, did, would not matter, could not. Had she placed her hand palm downward upon the candleflame, its pointed spiral might have pirouetted with prima-ballerina precision through the very palm-center, leaving only the most fragile puncture, opal-round, diamond-clear. And the paris-plaster mask above would have stared listlessly, hollow gaze unchanging.

"I'm married, Francina."

"I know. To Elizabeth. Congratulations. It's the most truthful thing, probably, that you've ever done."

Startled by this, he said, "What do you mean?"

Clipped, detached, she explained with patience: "You always worshiped her. Therefore, you wished to marry her. You wanted a wife you could *worship*. Your family wanted you to marry her. Everyone, including you, knew you'd marry Elizabeth. Only you never admitted it. Irrelevant, however, to anything that currently matters. I am not a psychoanalyst."

"What does matter?"

Francina thought: None of your damned business.

And politely said: "That also is irrelevant."

He knew it to mean: None of your damned business.

"May I ask you one thing, Francina?"

"You may ask."

"Why did you smile at me the way you did? Just outside the door?"

She had not expected the question, yet she heard it as if in a dream, answered with a vaguely ironic twist of the mouth and in a hollow, aloof voice:

"Because, Karl, now we can be friends—after a fashion."

"A fashion—like your magazines? I don't comprehend," he said.

"But that's why. Because, of course, you don't. And because this time you know it." With finality, she put out her cigarette, planted her dark glasses firmly upon her nose. "Just continue knowing and forget comprehending. I wouldn't, in your shoes, even consider such a thing as comprehension."

There being little more he could say, he paid the check and they returned to the street, each footfall having the clarity of a hanging-bell.

"May I walk you to work?" he asked. And received the casual, cordially-detached nod of acceptance.

"How's Roberta?" he said.

"Relatively well, I suppose."

"Only that?"

"She's been worse. She could do better."

"And what are you doing to help her?"

"What I have done isn't enough."

"Then do more, Francina."

"There is no more that I can do. No more. No less."

"I see."

Coolly: "You do not see. You should not bother pretending to. You *don't* live in that house, Karl."

"No, I suppose I don't."

Francina looked up, slightly wincing, as if from brash sunglare; but on Wabash Avenue, beneath the looming concrete and the ironwork of the vast "L" tracks, the glare was considerably diminished.

"It was nice to see you again, Francina."

Amiably, she replied: "Yes. Please give my regards to Elizabeth, and thanks for the lunch."

"My pleasure, Francina." Needing only a Victorian bow.

"Take it light and easy, Karl—etcetera."

"The same to you, Francina."

And like two well-run robots, they turned off, he down the street, and she into the revolving door.

With exception of a woman calling herself Mrs. Sill, who phoned asking if Monsieur Jean could manicure her poodle, the afternoon matched the morning.

"Monsieur," Francina told Mrs. Sill with the utmost tact, "is not licensed to hairdress or manicure pets. His professional aides are limited to slightly higher mammals—er—people. I am terribly sorry, madam."

After a sigh and giggle, Mrs. Sill told Francina she was sorry she hadn't thought of that, thanked her for being so nice, and hung up. Francina mentally added "y" to Sill, and flashed her best-patented smile at a departing customer who spent 5 hours per week in the salon and who regularly looked not one platinum hair-strand nor sequined eyelash better.

At 5:10 p.m., she was again upon the street, casually routed towards Michigan Avenue. Evenings she preferred to ride the bus without transferring. The subway was depressing then, and her 63rd and South Park transfer-point a step beyond. Against that milling, jangling intersection, polluted with stale cigarette butts and glass slivers, the city of Chicago had erected a grammar school, complete with schoolyard and basketball court. At first passings, Francina had felt almost physical horror of that dull-ruddy monument to the whims and depravities of the municipal power structure. But gradually it became a mere shadow, inadequate and pathetic—another gaunt gathering-place for the groping, wary black children bound within its district.

"Are we meant," Francina thought, "to always take more than we give? Funny if there be nothing left to take."

Sheltered behind her glasses, she scrutinized passing people: bearded, denim-clad artists clutching portfolios; 2 inches above-the knee-skirted-models, secretaries, and middle-society's newly-wed housewives; red-faced fighting-fiftyish flabby males with convention tags and pale-haired girls twenty years their junior; groups of matrons with well-sprayed champagne-gray hair and wide lace Peter-Pan collars on skimmer dresses; children—wiry, wide-eyed, wash'n'wear wrapped. In millenium, life passed by, crossing clown and automation, Hamlet and robot.

"And it's always been this way," Francina thought, turning as her bus skreeked to curb-stop. She dropped a quarter into the automatic coin-snatcher and slid into a window-side seat. Everyday she viewed the hotel and office buildings, shops and galleries—each time sighting something different: gray-clad black doormen at the Pick-Congress; a fringed velvet dress in Blum's Vogue with no price label; the costumed human advertisement in the Blue Angel's doorway; gypsy picture for auction at Building 600 Michigan So., sour-faced couple between pickle-colored curtains of the Essex Inn dining-room. Weary-eyed, she turned to her magazine.

At 24th and Michigan, enroute to South Parkway, the bus made a veering turn—mechanically, Francina caught at a railing. In quicksilver light-flash, the blue ring upon her hand glinted up at her. Sometimes she peered hard into its blue depths, secret-hunting. Perhaps its only secret (that it had been a gift of rare kindness) barely yet brushed her comprehension.

> "The honey-wind blows
> And the days grow colder.
> Somehow the years and I
> Grow a little bit older."

So pathetic to grow no wiser. Had the song's singer known? Maybe did or maybe not . . . how many ears had listened? Heard?

At Pershing Road, a haggard drunk, older than he should have been, stumbled upon the bus. His drab wool cap was frayed, cheap jersey shirt stained, trousers patched and baggy, his eyes were brightly vague. He fumbled his fare into the coin-snatcher, and staggered to the empty seat in front of Francina. He sprawled, muttering, chuckling.

Francina felt an unhappiness gnaw the edges of her serene self-isolation. This thing began with inability to push aside cocktails, leave bottles sealed. It seemed it had to swallow someone and anyone would do. She knew that at his corner bar he hadn't been a solo.

Quite suddenly, the man moved clumsily around in his seat, grinned leeringly at Francina. Sweat and stale whiskey-odor assailed her nostrils, her stomach turned a three hundred sixty degree somersault.

"Hey baby," he slurred. "Wha're doin' t'nig'd wid you foxy self?"

Automatically, Francina shrank far against the seat. In the next moment she was half-rising to move. But the man, clumsy-rising, said, "Aw baby, I ain' gonna hurt you—don' go . . . " And the bus hit uneven surface, jarring Francina further against the seat and the drunk man into the aisle at her feet, where he lay, mumbling curses and chuckling.

"He'p me," he pleaded, thrusting an arm in Francina's direction. A middle-aged lady across the aisle reached out in aid, but Francina silent-shivered sick and static. The driver had stopped the bus and risen, frowning, to attend to the situation.

"How far you going, mister?" demanded the driver, depositing him upon the side seat beside the door.

"Fo'ty sev'n street—I'm—I'm . . . "

"Well, never mind. Just sit still, please, and don't disturb the other passengers. I'll let you off at 47th."

"I'm . . ." the man called out pleadingly to Francina. She nodded and looked away, and the bus driver said firmly, "Let the lady alone, sir; she accepts your apology. But kindly let the lady alone."

The man nodded, mumbling, and looked pathetically at the floor.

Francina examined the fading sky and folded her arms hard against her stomach. Chill diffused her finger-veins, slithering reproachfully from half-mooned nails past her wristbones. A sunspot centered inch-distance of her lenses, lettering 400mg., skeletal reminder of equanil encounters ner-past.

At 47th Street, haggard and head bent, the man tottered awkwardly from the bus, and the only disgust left in Francina was for herself. Always the shrinking—from foul or harsh words, probing stares, clutching hands, even from dust against stair railings. Not from the mental recognition, simply from contact. With full awareness, she continued drawing further and further from the human reality.

At 63rd Street the bus filled. In accordance with her hopes, she saw no one she knew, and gazed absently out at the grammar school half-shadowed by "L" tracks. She, Francina Kerry, had learned to spell "cat" instead of "Kat" in a private elementary school where the kindergarten-thru-second-graders took afternoon naps on fuzzy rugs and where in the first grade, one girl was once absent for a month to go to Mexico with her parents and returned with tiny souvenirs for all of her classmates. She, Francina Kerry, who could touch without being touched, listen without hearing, see and not look. She, Francina, who remembered only what she chose not to forget, and said only what she cared to tell. She looked down at the clean blue cuffs of her blouse, at the snowy pleats of her skirt, at the barely scuffed tips of her white shoes—all yet neat, smart. A smoothly coiffed mannequin with long, lacquered nails, and a plaster-coated mold half-hidden behind large black sunglasses. And she knew that she, in typical cowardly fashion, had made her own choice, and must exist responsible for it—to it. In any way or another must pretend to play prefabricated tunes—even during miscellaneous recall by a 1/10 offbeat bend in her foot.

Off the bus, Francina walked drag-footed in the direction of the Kerry house. Quiet street, even with the cries from children on bicycles, or playing tag. Quiet even when someone down the street gave a double JW party and someone else called the disorderly conduct wagon. Quiet even when the harsh voices of Laura and Joseph Kerry distinctly could be heard from the alley behind their house.

Francina walked more slowly, and her head and shoulders drooped.

Yet, life revolved, with the merciless infinity of all master clockwork.

Her head, that ached from being held so arrogantly, seemed more painful lowered. Halting suddenly, Francina stiffened her shoulders, set her chin, and pointed her nose in the air a full half-inch higher than before.

"Time," she thought, "Waits for nothing and no one."

Had she once been foolish enough to imagine it might wait for her?

Again she willed her mind to semi-vacancy, her face and voice to mechanical, polite amiability.

At the doorstep, she fit her key into the lock, turned it, pushed open the door. All just as she'd left it — stale and tense—heavy with temporarily silent cries of chronic malcontent and frustrations —and the curtains still knotted in the windows, marking Laura's choice of outlet after 20 years.

"Well, hi," said Laura Kerry. "How did it go today?"

"Oh, quite the same as usual," Francina replied.

"You look strained and tired. Are you sure you feel all right?"

"Quite certain, Mother."

"See anyone interesting in town? Anyone new or anyone you knew?"

Francina's eyes flew to the ring upon her finger, and a strange nausea tugged at her stomach. Still detached and withdrawn, she replied absently, "Not really, and I wasn't looking for anyone."

"Ohh . . . " a somewhat amused chuckle at her daughter's bored sarcasm. Then—"your father wouldn't say when he'd be back, so we can have dinner anytime you like. Roberta hasn't come in from dancing, either."

"Oh," Francina said, "Well, she'll be around soon . . . ' '

"Hmph."

"I'll cook dinner." Francina had started toward the stairs.

"No need. It's a roast; it and the trimmings are already done."

The telephone rang.

"Hel-lo!" said Laura Kerry. "Uh—yes, who's *calling*, please?" Several pitches louder: *"Hi Tony,* how're you? Just a moment—Francina! Tony Merchant's on the phone! OK?"

Oh. OK . . . Tonight's date . . . Tony-the-tin-toned-lady-trap,, self-styled playboy of Kappa world . . . you'll do. Nothing else to do today. Dance, drink, blase . . . OK . . . Francina, halfway up the stairs, wandered down again, absently took the receiver from her mother's hand.

"Hey, Tony."

"Hi doll . . . "

Fragment Reflection I
(thru smokescreen)

An orphan, yes. But not
an orphan, pale against
my uncle's foot and
spear. We wait below
a sunburnt sky to scale
the hill, hunt the stars.
Hold the lion's mane
and kiss his bearded
roar.

Reckoning A.M. Thursday After an Encounter
Between a Sawdust Sack and a Silly

1

Murder self slowly. And die like ants shuffling up under
Jolly Green's
        (foot.)?
Or his ass, what the hell, it all amounts to same if she
don't know if he don't know *how* they don't know—Which
        they don't
And won't while she pays the laundry for his pussy-stained
pants (and *he* calls *her* the "whore":
        Dig, man—if she give you some lip I'll turn you
        on the "fly"—I had that bitch the second night)
        said Cooky the amateur cockhound . . .
        . . . and out the other side his flip-top-trap—(Don't
        be fuckin' with my *woman,* you cats, 'cause *she* ain't
        had nobody but me & she got to raise them 12 kids I
        plan to bless (! ?) with my name) . . .

Tabled. Specimen trapped for research. Curious-eyed they
poke & prod, desperately hunt *their* concept of flaw . . .
Marbles gaping *were* her eyes. Voices from a place in time—
    "How can you *have lovers?*"
      —Make me out a freak? All have bi-sexual urges.
"Not urges. Not *women.* Women have babies."
      —I don't.
"How don't you??"
      —Will. And the Pill. Thank *someone's* god.
"Oh my God!! I didn't get you pregnant!!"
      —Hell no foolish nigger. You ain't dumping your
      17th brat down *this* hole.

2

    "you don't look well."
      (What you care? Liar.)
    "Are you sure you're all right?"
      (What-the-fuck-you-care. Liar.)
    "I'll talk to you tomorrow
baby
      (Go 'head on, nigger. We both got what you
      came & I let you in my door for.)
Go 'head on 'cause I got a woman 'cross town. Used
to be yours—you thought—she knew better. Bought
her that canary dress you wouldn't, fearing other dudes
would look too hard. They look. I look too. She
looks *also,* & back at me.

2.5

Only the "Bitch," well-used to others' filthy labels, stayed—
To jam a bullet up the crack in Cooky's ass & fish his lady's
face from greasy dishwater & detergent cracking & splitting
her skin . . .
    . . . Where were women-men-men & women? Ever were there?
      Men?
And Women? . . .
      . . . Or only blood & billysticks and whippinst (d)icks for

wedding nights (as "proof" of (e) mas-cu-li-ni-ty) . . . and
squalling kids with little love, trained as automation (s) by
parents with no love at all, ever, for each other . . .
. . . Where were women-men-men & women? Ever were there?
      Men?
And Women? . . .
. . . Ever did a man exist whose eyes and hands were tender?
Whose face lit sighting a frilly-frosted party cake? Talked
with his woman, not at or above her? Ever did a woman come un-
scheming for money or muscles? Uncringing uncondemning nor
shamed if *he* cried (& if she were an engineer, still did her
lover love her?) . . .
. . . Where were women-men-men & women? Ever were there?
      Men?
And Women? . . .
      Only fags deserve respect.

3

Sanitariums. didn't cure. People. didn't go. Nor doctors. go to
people—with any worthmore than "dolls" and broken tinkertoys.
Dead and dying (Dust) In their tombs of mud & gore. Mausoleums
of decaying lust . . . Learning. too late. couldn't nothing come
with them—not there. Inscription reading:
      Wouldn't wash (ourselves)
      We lied. We died.

3.5 + infinity

Let's split. Let's split.
I know a beach where we can go. Wars are over. We can go.
We're dying and they're dead . . .
. . Let's split . . hold hands and trip the track through
swirling silvered sand and water clear like foaming crystal . . .
. . . We will never go back . . .
Hell was there on earth.
I'll pin a lotus in your (hair . . .

CARL CLARK

No More

I am a river.
My course is freedom.

I am the tide
Eroding the ignorant-rocks.

I am time
Moving on.

I am the wind
Blowing the songs of change.

My hair curls sharply.
My nose is flat.

I am black.
I celebrate,
I damn your gods,
And thank you too.

Conundrum

I am my prison;
Encapsuled in my biases,
Caught up in my fevers,
Tightly bound by my loves

And holding all who love me
(I entrapped them with honeyed
words and dollars hung on weeks.)

Leave while you can
Before the ties grow too tight.
I cannot free you.
I am inside myself.

(Thoughts from a Bottle)

I have a bottle and a pen
To separate the yan and the yin.
The shadow and the substance.
The was, the is, and the will be.

What benign God created this paradise?
Or
What mad God made this hell?

Can I
With the ju ju of my words
Wrench this madman's spell
And bring
One lucidity
One thought
Finer than gossamer
Trembling like a hot woman
(And nebulous as her love,
But sweet oh so sweet
wisdom!
Open up your legs!)

Wantonly I pursue the yan
A bitch called Knowledge
And the yin
A whore called poetry.
I have paid your fee, whore,
And now I sing.

Allegory in Black

The bright white street lights
shine, reflect, shine.
Shine of the dirty white snow
making of it a garish stage.

Wine bottles policy slips
sweepstake tickets war medals
and unemployment applications
litter the stage like tinsel.

A jukebox sends the song of the Bird
soaring high and lonely
phrasing out his frustration, his loneliness,
his desire to be real,
to dream.
The drummer picks up the refrain,
kicks to crescendo, and crashes to
dissonant reality.

And the wind blows
blows down dirt roads to sharecroppers' shacks;
over cracked pavement to tenements;
along stately avenues to highrise apartments;
through proletarian poverty
and middle class myopia.
The wind blows,
calling forth the actors
huddled backstage.
To joust the stereotype.
To chase the dream.
The Pied Piper of the dream.

II

Our first actor is kicked on stage from a slaver;
The wind blows cold and white;
It strips him of tradition and identity.
Disperses his family.
Strips his children's memories
of Heritage,
and pride.
Chains his limbs. (In the land of the free).
Shackles his mind.
He struggles violently as Nat Turner.
As John Greene.
Cries as Dred Scott.

Temporizes as Booker T. and Mary Mc.
Laughs bitter laughter as Plessy vs Ferguson.
    And the wind blows.
He and his multiply.
They spread across the face
of "one nation under God."
They walk the byways
and habitat the backdoors.
They chase the dream
and watch the river
And the snow; and the night,
The cold bleak night
Stretching across three centuries.
A night filled with terror
With hurt;
With frenetic acts of genocide
against the body politic.
A night filled with the sound of a people
running from the wind.
The wind that hangs.
That imprisons;
that plays the melody. of the dirty white snow
and the melody of the dream.

III

And the cold white wind blows
Spewing forth the vultures
The white vultures:
The black vultures:
The yellow vultures;
The tenement vultures:
The 'no-money-down' vultures:
The 'go-slow' vultures.
And the seekers of dreams.
Dreams for the weed
Dreams from the needle
Dreams from the bottle
Hair straightener
Lip thinner

Nose pinchers
Magic charms and bleaching cream.
Uncle Thomas politicians
Reeking of oil from the party machine,
And peddling the nostrum of the dream.
Regurgitate.
      Regurgitate the wind.

IV

  Traumatized from cradle to hangman's noose
Given stars he cannot reach;
given a dream not to his use;
Hungry in a land of plenty;
Barefooted in a forest of shoes
Standing Black and bitter
In a white world of glitter
Weaned on promises and
committees-to-talk-it-over
Discriminated and tolerated
segregated and hated.
Mind forged in a psychological crucible
body toughened by the wind.
Begging no more,
'Boy' comes of age
to have the dream.
Moves to have it now
Or strip away its gaudy facade
And let it die.

Ode to A Beautiful Woman

You do not know how beautiful you are.
You cannot see your skin,
Beautiful burnished brown-black
Catching the rays of an autumn sun;
Reflecting more than is.

You cannot taste the honey that is your lips
Curved so beautifully,
Or see the curves I would trace
With gentle finger tips.

In my mind all summer I held your face.
Now we stand close to each other
And I am without voice.
Perhaps you can hear another
Like the beat of my heart
Or the touch of my hand.

What would I give
For the softness of your arms?
Sunlight and sorrow,
Spring and tears.
All that was
More than is.

But you are more than sweetness and beauty.
You are flame.
Burning brightly, burning brown.

Come close, warm me, even
If I die in the flame.

The Second Coming

It came
Out of the blackness of the spaces between galaxies.
Out of the exploding unity of creation.
Out of sixty million years of racial memory.
It hung in the sky over the delta, shining, twinkling.
It hung there for three days and three nights.
And all the world raised its eyes
To the thing in the blackness
The star blocker.
On the third day it began to fall.
It fell with a high keening sound
Like the weeping of a lost soul
Or a forsaken God
And Malcolm and Aski
And Lopez and Smith,
And King and Caruso
And Lewis and O'Brian
and Pious and Don
and Solomon and Johnson,
and Pogo and Bertram
Laid down their works and went thither
And the chosen did see visions
and dreamt of the Second coming of the Nazarene
And when the wise men gathered together the Chosen said,
"He comes!"
And on the second day when the churches were filled
and the ministers sat with Rabbis
and the Priests with the Preachers
And they beat their breasts
and tore out their hair
And fell upon their knees
And did Pray.
And the Faithful said
"He comes!"
And on the Third day
Those that held others in bondage
Held them no more.

And those that killed
Murdered no more.
And those that robbed,
Stole no more.
Those that lay with another's wife
Cast their seeds forth no more in sin
And covered their bodies with sack cloth and ashes
And wept and adultered no more
Only the liars lied
(Lest civilization perish)
And the weepers wept
(Lest man die)
And the chosen dreamed dreams
And walked in all manner of high and lonely places
And said, "He comes!"
On the Seventh day He comes
And the Shining Twinkling fell
Like a thing without weight
Or a God walking to His Crucifixion
On the Fourth day the people saw the Cross
Looming larger than the universe
On the fifth day the Faithful saw the Crown of Christ
And the drops of blood falling in the holy blackness of space
And those that believed in the Nazarene did pray
And those that believed not
Did believe
And nations turned their bombs to plow shares
And their swords to hoes
The wolf slept with the lamb
And all things did flourish
Even the seas stilled
And waited His coming
On the Sixth day the Chosen dreamed dreams
And walked in Terrible and Lonely places
And said, "He comes!"
"With the nailprints,
"He comes!"
And bowed under some horror beyond ken
Prostrated themselves before Him

And bled from His wounds
And shared His knowledge
And died from it
And the people saw the nailprints
And knelt before Him
And sent up Psalms and paeans of praise
To the Son of the Mother
Of God's only begotten child
And His voice rolled out
Like the thunder of mighty rockets
And the cooing of gentle doves.
I am the God of the Old Testament and the New
Of Moslem and the Jew
The Mohammedan and the Hindu
Of the Christian Scientist and Adventist
Of the Marxist and Leninist
Catholicism and Protestantism
And Father divine, are mine
And the sinners and the saved,
I am He who caused midnight at noon
Cured the sick,
Raised up the dead
And walked on the waters
I turned water to wine
And fed the Multitudes
With a loaf of bread
I cured the lepers
And brought the gift of eternal life
From my Father God Almighty.
I came as I come now
As one of the most oppressed
And they rejected me and you rejected me
And placed on my head
This crown of thorns
And pierced my body
With nails and spikes
And hung me on the Cross to die a slow and lingering death
A slow and lingering death
Will you reject me again?

And the dead cried
"No, Son of the living God."
And the living cried
"Neither in this world nor the next will we forsake THEE"
Will we forsake THEE
And the animals that walked on the land
And swam in the sea
And soared in the wind
Gave too their troth.
And He said
"So spake those who lined the roads to Calvary"
Even unto my disciples.
One betrayed me
for thirty pieces of silver.
Another denied me three times
Before the cock crew twice.
And those who worshiped with me
lined the path to cast stones and rubbish upon me
And only the Cyrene came to help me with my cross
And the burden of your sins
Though I could not hate you mocked me
Though I could not die you crucified me
And my blood washed your sins away
Yet in my name you have pillaged and raped
Tortured and Exploited
And spread the love of my Father with death
And smallpox and syphilis
You have raised magnificent edifices and idols in my name
But you have spurned my poor and my dispossessed
You are forgiven
I bless those who are reborn
And those who have never lived
I baptize all those who hear in the name of the living God
I stop Ahasuerus from wandering
I stop Sam from hanging
I take the guilt of my Chosen and my Deputy
I forgive my dissenters and splinters
I sanctify all unions made in my name.
Let all who spread my word be ordained

Let all who believe be saved
Let the crippled walk
Let the sick be healed
and the weary rested.
These things I do in the name of the Father and the Son and the
    Holy Ghost.
And the words of the Nazarene glittered.
On the Seventh day it landed
And walked the world
And touched the heart of every man and every beast
And the earth rose up to form an altar
At the place of his coming.
And the dirt turned to gold
And the rainbow framed the altar
All the birds of the air gathered above him
And the peoples of the Delta gathered there to welcome the Christ
And they hated not and did laugh
And were brothers one to the other
And then they saw the Son of the Blessed Virgin
And they that had been sick cast stones.
Those that were crippled threw their crutches and garbage.
Those who killed no more, killed
Those who robbed no more, stole and adultered.
And nations took out their plow shares and hoes
and made bombs and swords.
For the Savior indeed came as the oppressed.
He came with flowers in his hair.
He came BLACK.
Out of their love
Christians screamed
"Jew!"
And the Jews screamed
"False Messiah!"
And the death-dealers
and the exploiters
cried "Charlatan!"
And the blacks shouted
"Slave dealer! Honky!"
And the cross was

worshiped in flame.
And the Christ was
Crucified and buried.
On the third day.
Man died.

PEGGY SUSBERRY KENNER

Image in the Mirror

me nappy hair dream child
sending Father's Day cards
to the cemetery
to sow
unseasoned sour soil.

i left son of Davie
where all the buffalo hunters
should be—
in a coma—
jumping over/on
picked diet faced whores
and eating white berries
when found.

unclenched hostilities
i hurry
to hear four faces cry
all blooming bubble blowers
 with pink poppy ribbons and
candle eyes/love child/children
unchained from shame—
what/when will you begin
being.

regurgitate little ones
with enthusiasm
applaud not makers of
processed foods
canners of gasoline to spray
at you—as sloven slavemasters
would have you.
Malcolm X
gave you vacuum cleaner and
melodies—with style—
now erupt enuresis

echo for your cause.
i hear a new hymn
>(who stole the cookies from the cookie jar
>the hunkies stole the cookies from the
>cookie jar
>who me?
>yes you—
>number one.)

royalty murmurs
a growing budget is yet uncurbed
unbudded roses cut off in prime
i know a good dump sight
contributions should go to
>america
>369
>washington, d.c.

(2)

my Black man
my sho nuf Black man
what was once frigid
now lingers
fatigued
in a flaming form
from your fragile caresses
carefully cherished
in my
blossomed bosom of Blackness/
i
your boomerang
u
thunderbolt my tremor.

U had your first communion
wore dashiki as twaddlers wore
tuxedos
i proud you connected to
my umbilical cord
if u never receive fringe benefits

from advocates for toms
and
the caricatured zombies with
parrot fever
do not make u
house nigger
i will not mind
u be long stranger
"hi ho silver."

Done told me once to
wane—in a
Black direction
at 26 and 2 i had my
coming out party
the deb wore Black
and white African printed dress
the ivory bone was taken
from my head and nose
and
"i feel good."

No Bargains Today

waz, adverse to thinking
got transplant
Glear, Glance, Peer—
sales prices
swaggered bargains

Jim has,
pamphlets—records—
mental exchanges

today's sales
(dehydrated bananas
dehydrated pig-ears
dehydrated pig-feet

                              dehydrated mustard greens and
                                    ham hocks)

a sale—a sale—
zoom
      exodus
            push
for today only
red/white/blue
self cleaning oven
burns clean in few hours

                              let it burn the cracks of
                              time
                              i can use it to
                              barbecue the rats and roaches

"economize with gas"
"gas does the big jobs better"
"millions are cooking with gas"

                              savory glazed shacks
                              supreme stuffed stores that
                              greased off the
                              western controlled Blacks
                              got caught cooking their steaks
                              in black iron skillets with
                              brandy sauce for a topping

someone lit
a
match
that steak had to burn
itself out
in
Chicago, Detroit, L.A. and
more more more
to come.

                              the window of happiness got
                              cracked up

came

down like
snow storm of salvation
crumbling Christ with
crusts from the
corpus de-lic-ti

the glass
gleaming glazed
synthetic hopes of

catching up with
loo-la Bell—
anna Bell—
susie Bell—
all the Bells that came to
america on
a cracker
eating roots and gravel
eating sperm of
people—pushing them in
fly patch of
insecticide—that
milked emptied breast of
aging women—to the sound of

the liberty Bell
ringing/did not ring/
V Day over poverty Bell
the bomb was sent
spreading germs over ghetto life
whiter than you
dropped it

caught a sale on refrigerators
got frozen trying to
drag it home.
little spider caught in web
trying to get bottles of
super-cider.
Knocked down flag polls of

                              investigations to see WHY . . .?
                              a field goal attempted

zoom—exodus
push—prey—
on the predators that

                              digested you
                              auctioned you
                              made you
                              rain-bow
                              sam-bow
                              knee-bow

today unattainable
today unacceptable
today unreliable

                              tomorrow will give you
                              "Karate—with mint"
                              "Arrid—extra dry"
                              a soundless shavemaster
                              a shoe horn for bare feet (if)
                              you bes good

unrobe—
uncover—
rap
sisters listening cause
brothers saying
and dying

                              legislature listening
                              passed new bill for more
                              police.

the establishment says
bear heads
face of wool
bleak/bleak/bleak
sheep and reBels/REBELS/

attune
the colleges threw the chickens
out
they say, you
tainted, tangy, full of turmoils
no parcels and
no sales.

no matter
got
roped mops and
gray matter

unleash—Blacker than you
smarter than me
finer than you
got more money than me
from that
corked catch-up bottle.

Comments

sighted a Black tornado of
flying feces
polluting
pollinating towards
Black leaders
it zeroed in from
air-conditioned rooms
            surveillance/surveillance
the FBI done rapped and tapped
King/Clay and the Honorable one
            surveillance/surveillance
don't touch that phone
sighted a
illegitimate Black baby

they sprayed it with
white paint
and
insecticide

now all
disavow
any knowledge
of
illegitimacy.

The Round Table

The round table will not tell.
You can preach or teach.
Pass the coffee and cake.

Minds generate like genesis.
Business is not always orderly.
Liberation, conversation, revolution
exchange.
Pass the soul, please.

Spokesmen, spokeswomen spoon-fed us.
Someone took my tea bag and handed me
a sponge.

The table is omnipotent.
You become richer from brief encounter.
Speak, speak
editors, innovators, writers, speak.

All shades of blackness are purged,
as Africa dangles before us from
the literature of absent brothers,
and sisters, who
left their literature and pamphlets.

Invigorating;
inspiration,
a spiritual seance.

Agree or disagree; conjured voices from
mystic sepulchers make their appearances.
Filtering into the smoky room, echoing,
coming into cosmos.
Hands are clasped,
chained together.
Members and visitors have
visitations.
It is your turn to carry the ball.
Touchdown.
And no one
leaves the round table.

Black Taffy

my life
is
a
bald headed match
that has
not been
struck

           Chicago's broken glass kept
           greens from growing near
           the crowded tenements that
           absorbed sunlight from
           cribs

fairy tales and
stargazing
white teacher had me
trying to fill cracks
in moon

           bloom-ing
           slowly
           perceiving concepts of
           civilization

                              i
                              got stung
                              trying to
                              concentrate
concentration/concentration/
"Fun with Dick and Jane"
who is Jane?
i want my
pig-meat

                              memories
                              i forgot my
                              name
                              tried to remember
                              the first
                              pale finger that
                              pointed and said
                              i
                              was in error
                              whenever/wherever
                              i
                              was

locked in a
closet
frightened by
dark-places
dark-people
with
white faces

                    (2)

straggling/straggling
spirits talk to me in
dreams
that were still visual
when i awakened
on the full
moon
from my coffin
'66

i found snake
separated and
disgorged it
put pieces in
cesspool
saw again isolated
in picture frame
saying—

    (hell is rotating
    down dried insect infested
    slimy murky holes to
    no where so
    u.s.a. can
    keep image)

    (heaven is
    not going)

14 set off
optic nerve of
the finger pointers when
they
burned his
keep sakes

i remembered on t.v.
you remembered i wash clothes/
use soap/gasoline/clean house/
buy toothpaste/clean toilets/
after 400 years i'm a t.v. star
got look of "vogue" with
long doughnut doe-doe curls

(3)

i can be served a
hot dog in
the front alley
i can buy your house
after
it's sighted for
slum clearance

Panthers too slow
to catch
pussy-cats
leaving
the police stands

                    statue of
                    liberty too
                    short
                    to hold
                    torch on/over
                            (peeping john
                            john the
                                    got u on t.v.
                            john the
                                    rap
                            john the
                                    tap
                            john the
                                    sentence makers)

sentencing u to
more years at
hard labor for
singing

                    "we
                    shall
                    over
                    come"

Memories of the Long Seat

(Dedicated to Sharon Scott and my Children)

I was just seven or eight when I took my first trip to a down south state. Mom had dressed me up in my Sunday best, with white socks and black patent leather shoes that pinched my toes. Mom thought I looked "cute." Had my bad Easter hat on in the middle of July. The wide navy blue hat almost covered the scabby burn that sat out on one ear. A Chicago beautician had fried my ear and cooked out half of my hair.

New Orleans was our stop, but we had a chance to pass through Mississippi. Now I'm glad we just passed it. When we got to New Orleans I met my aunt and most of my kin. I saw palm trees and went places I had never been before. At the show the usher escorted us to the balcony. I had never sat in the balcony before. It seemed like such fun to look down on everything. When we were leaving I saw a water fountain bubbling. I ran to get a drink but couldn't reach it so I asked my aunt to give me a boost. "No baby, the colored folks' water is over there." "But I don't want no colored water." I kept trying to reach the fountain by myself. Mom came over and pulled me away by my arm. She was mad. "Now mind your manners, child, and do as you are told." She turned to my aunt and said how embarrassed she was. Better to be embarrassed than thirsty, I thought; but then, I had never been able to figure out grown-ups.

My aunt said we could take a bus home. I was glad because I liked buses. We had old red street-cars in Chicago. I saw the red, white and blue bus coming. "Goodie goodie!" I jumped on the bus smiling and happy and sat on the long seat right behind the driver. Mom gave me a funny look and motioned for me to follow her, but I just sat and watched her move to the rear and move some sort of little sign. I smiled back at the faces that started looking at me. It was my big hat, I thought. It sure was a hot day for hats. Mom motioned for me to come again. I shook my head and started to look away when she said, "You come here, chil', and sit by me." My aunt had left me the seat next to mom but I didn't want to sit on the end. Besides, from my seat I could see everything. I start- ed to leave my seat, but not without making a face and going into

104

my protest act. Before I could get my feet to moving mom had stormed over and she had that arm again. She gave me a headache in my arm and two headaches in my feet, from dragging me out of that seat. I never could figure out grown-ups. They make a federal case out of a long seat.

Life in My Own Dust

One day Mom said to me "You know, Tonja, when you was small I just prayed and prayed you wouldn't come up with no baby like all them other girls was doing. Child, as I see you now in yo fur coat and glitter, I wonders. I wonders if I ain't prayed wrong. There's worser things can happen to a girl. Things like you doing, child. Things mom don't even like to talk 'bout." Her voice began to plead. "I know you like pretty things. But don't you see, child . . . things don't count . . . It's yo soul that counts."

* * * *

People were always asking "Is that your daughter?" It was always with a note of surprise. Mom would smile proudly, beaming with joy at her acknowledgment of me. I never knew why they asked her until I began to hear things like "ain't no way in the world you can tell me that child belongs to that woman. If it is so, that child's daddy must be white. Honey, you don't tell me 'cause I know 'bout it. She 'bout done laid up somewhere with some hunky and got herself that child. Might be some of them white folks she work for. You know how that go." I was twelve when I heard that kind of talk. I cried about it then. I never told mama.

Old Katie Shaw was head of the big mouth brigade. She was one of those people that couldn't say anything good about anybody. "Sister McNear," she said to mama one day, "you's still a young woman. Better get yo'self somebody to hep you raise yo daughta. You know how fas these youngns is nowadays. Can't tell'm nothin. They all runnin round talkin bout dresses and being hip. With them goof-off pills and all." Her face looked positive. Like it knew everything. "It just scares me," she went on. "No wonder so many of them comin up with babies and stuff. And they showing everything today. Ain't covering nothin. It's destroyin' the youth. Don't leave nothin fur the young boys to think bout. Everythin right out in the open fur everybody to see. And the way them gals sit down on the buses. I'm afraid to look."

It made me sick to hear Katie Shaw talk. She never knew when to shut up. "I know you heard 'bout Sister Sarah's daughta," Katie would go on. "Hear what?" mama asked. "She done got herself a baby." Katie got happy explaining that. "Just turned fourteen. Didn't finish gramma school." Katie Shaw looked at me. "How old's Tonj now?" "Oh . . . she's almost fourteen," mama said. "Yeah," Katie said, continuing to look at me. "Well, Sister McNear, you just mind what I said and think about it. "Ain't nothin to think about," mama said. "God gave me one good man and took him. I don't guess I'd be that lucky to find another good husband. If the Lord wanted me to have a husband, I spect he'd sent him by now."

That old Katie was always grinning in mama's face. Supposedly giving her advice. Then she would get outside in the summer, hanging up her children's dingy clothes, and talk about mama. How mama carried her Bible around like some saint. How she thought she was better than the rest of the women on that block. (Just because mama didn't sit around and drink beer, and gossip about everybody in the block.)

One day I forgot my books and returned home. I heard old Katie and some other bag discussing the check mama got every month. "I don't think Sister McNear ever been married," Katie said. "That child she got don't look nothing like her." "Well, you can't go by that," the other woman said," 'cause I got some kids that don't look like me too, and I got some real light folks in my family. Some of um even look kind of white like Mis' McNear's child. . . . Way these folks is all mixed up and all . . . You just can't say that, Miss Katie." "Well if that's her child I bet the daddy ain't colored. . . . Now that' all I'm go say 'bout it." "But Miss Katie," the other lady went on, "we got everything in our race. I know you done seen the folks that could pass." "All I knows is she gets some sort of check in the mail," Katie went on. "I'm sure it ain't from aid 'cause she don't have no worker comin round. The name on that check ain't McNear." Old Katie was pointing her definite finger at the other woman and making all of her positive gestures. "That check got a different name on it too. I can't read all the name. But I been tryin to see it befo the mailman put it in the box. Now she sure nuf goes by the name of McNear, but the name on that check starts with a D." "Could it be Dallas?" the other woman interrupted. Old Katie's eyes widened. She had discovered something. "Yes . . . Yes. That's prob'ly it," she cried. "A truant officer was here one day asking fur-rh-ah Dallas. I told um weren't no one in this building by that name."

At first I had just wanted to listen. Just to hear what they had to say. I couldn't take it; so I interrupted the ladies. I told fat Katie off. Went right up to her. "Cow!" I said. And I said a lot of other things that I can't remember now. I was damn mad.

Old Katie should have been a prize fighter. Rough-looking. Evil-looking. No female graces at all. Her teeth looked like cave formations—all decayed. From the corrosion on them you would have thought she chewed tobacco or dipped. And— I never saw that woman once when her mouth wasn't in motion. No doubt she talked in her sleep. That habit she had of shaking her stubby fat finger in you made you want to scream. Bad also were those rolls of flabby fat shaking on her arms, and the awful odor that came from her arm pits. She had such a variety of bad smells. I didn't think she brushed, washed, or even wiped after anything. I was just glad she never shook her leg at me. Those kids of hers must have been the result of test tubes.

I often thought about mama and the years we spent in the flat over the tavern. Especially when life seemed hard for me. I would fantasize, sometimes, that we lived in one of the fancy high-rise buildings, instead of over the smelly old tavern that was a hang-out for the local misfits. The smell of piss was always in the halls . . . the community bathroom was never kept clean. Some drunk was always parking himself on the stairs and taking a leak. The dimly-lit stairway often revealed a couple engaged in petting or rhythmic intercourse. One night I came upon such a couple, sprawled out on the stairs. "Excuse me," I murmured. The man's breathing became more profuse with the girl's groans. The girl sounded distressed. One leg extended upward toward the railing. I stood there trying to figure out what to do. All I could think of was getting in before mama. I made three steps over the couple's head. They never stopped. Either they did not know I was there or they did not give a damn. I thought that all men certainly must be half goat and women like her half horse. I saw what they were doing but couldn't figure out what the purpose was. That night I decided to ask mama. She sat me down and told me of those things it was her duty to call "worldly." One sentence mama said stayed with me. "You don't want to be that type, Tonja. Them's street women."

Lucky thing mama died. Lucky thing mama can't see me now.

CAROLYN RODGERS

Jump Bad

Do y'all remember when you was in grammar school during recess or lunchtime out on the playground. And uh hole bunch of the boys and girls from yo room would be laughing and talking and signifying wid each otha. And somebody, sooner or later would start talking bout somebodies mama, but this particular time its yo mama. And they would say something so smart it would make you reallll mad. And everybody would be laughing bout you and yo mama.
And the one who did the signifying would say to you—

>you don't like it?
>you wanna JUMP BAD about it?

And you would say yeah (maybe) and you would start crying an sniffing and wiping yo nose and feelings on you coatsleeves and pretty soon y'all be in uh circle circling round each otha and then you be so mad you put up yo dukes and FIGHT.

>yeah.

Well the hunkie signifies with our lives. Caps all over our mamas. And our papas. And we dun shoved our fists in his face so much we dun showed most of our hand.

Remember those playground days when we was some badddddd motorfreeters who knew how to even up scores. Remember them. Cause us Black Folk is gonna have to sho'nuff JUMP BAD to git ourselves liberated from this hunkie.

"In This House, There Shall Be No Idols"

i would not tell them why i had smashed the window with my
hand. i had never known my blood was so red.

the little chips decorated my
skin and it glittered an expensive jewel.

the day was gray on blue and the sun came out every now and
then, to let the world know it was still on the case. the street
was almost empty except for two or three people standing
out fronting off the chicken shack. i could smell
the chicken frying through the air.

he's nasty and he drinks all the time and his wino friends hang out
around the newsstand. the gray steel newsstand smooth cool clean,
friendly if you like sterility, pissed in, baptized regularly.

he has no place to piss and he drinks so much his bladder
must be weak; he just uses the stand for a toilet. i tell
you the de-cent christians around here are sick of 'im.
sometimes he be so drunk you can't even get a paper
from 'im and sometimes you got to wait ten fifteen
minutes until he gets back from somewhere.

he's always begging for a dime or quarter too . . .
what time does the bank close? dressed in blue like a regular
policeman, forty colored years a fat middle with gold honored
teeth and wide flat feet.

lady i don't know, why don't you ask the man over there, he's
been working here since he was a little boy—bout thirty years. he
knows everything bout this bank.

color-ed. back bent, body like the cupped hand holding wine
or water, (now tell me, did jesus really serve) only the wise sur-
vive/
washing bannisters gold like teeth and scrubbing marble
floors fifty years if a minute
jesus. the beginning & the end.
the bank rolled on as the green rolled in.
no. i would not tell.

. . . you say you want to pass this test huh?
well, you'll do just fine. you do a favor for me, i'll do one for
you, what'd you mean you can drive why you almost hit that
curb, just lay the money on the seat, baby, nice pair of legs you
got there too here put your telephone number on this form too.
just kidding ha ha ha . . . can't you people take a joke? a joke?
a joke? a joke?

everybody drives

what good is pride and no car to drive, important things to do . . .
who ever invented pride anyway.
this here child of mines is got too much pride. one of these
days she'll lose it/ain't nothing but false pride anyway.
mama, where does pride come from?

and there he was. yes. sitting in the back
of the church, sitting on the paper flat to
the green wall high priest his hair covering
his shoulders all yellow as the sun and the
blue eyes deeper than any sky and cheaper
than the paint and the long white robe and
the white lamb and the brown rod or staff

that will lead led lose and the
sign was printed kidergarten style black
crayons said jesus never fails wait on the
lord, wait wait the sun was out the earth
was rising in me and i smelled the ground
of me and i heard the answer the glass was

thin and me so strong stronger sweat rolling
like syrup squeezed from the yam i heard the
answer and the spirit moved me moved me yes
i moved uh hum and i moved uh hum yes i did . . .

i did not tell them why i broke the window.
when they came.
i had spaced.

Phoenix

I

off the track
i blew
and traveled with the wind
howling
there were many voices—
screaming blooddrops of time

now, flown from the circles
and sound
there is only one tone mine
but i have lost hearing
to the wind, many voices,
and cannot remember
where to listen.

II

a silence is re-flowing
the peace that roars
inner beauty
the beat of your pulse
is lost in the
howling of the wind
i am returning—phoenix—
cradling creation in the
silences.

and i shall
travel with the wind
no more.

Jazz

three of us
in the bar
was red shimmering
and a willow weeping blue
and the glasses clicked and clinked
and the murmur of thick mouths
made the moan/song sound.
then the lady
        spinning

sides, played a trip
to the sun
blu-bla-wheeeeeeeeee
splu-du-m dahhhhhhhhh

tapped the sounds in our heads,
trapped the words in our mouths
bombed the air/scooped the thoughts
blu-bla-wheeeeeeeeeee
splu-du-m dahhhhhhhhhhhh
and the bar
blu bla wheeeeeeeeee was
red splu du-m dahhhhhhh and a
screaming weeping sound
three of us
        splu-du-m dahhhhhhh
        blu-bla-wheeeeeeeee
        wah wah weeeeeeeeeeeeeeeeee

Rebolushinary x-mas/eastuh julie 4/etc. etc. etc. etc.

yeah.
you can really
tell where

a people is at
on nation al
holi day times.
riding walking
standing staring
into through the
negro (sic) black
neighborhoods
seeing all the
fat white men
jumping out uh them
red bags
and the yellow-haired baby dick
with mary (jane) still slim (diet cola & such no doubt)
blue shy eyes applepiety as (n) ever
and the moo moos
MILITANTLY guarding
hippie joe and her from
hark! (is that uh wise)
dark skin we see!!!
bearing jewels from
someplace in the stars
near/where we now
oughta be goin
But—
Talkin
to people everyday
Black, they are
i know them
we talk the same ways
believe, i am told, similar dreams.
and yet,
why
do they say to me
    "my heart ain't in it, i'm just goin through the motions
besides,
i'm only celebrating it
FUH THE CHILDREN
and i'm sayin yeah,

that's precisely what i'm talkin
about
THE CHILDREN
and who
breathes life into new dreams
when everybodys hanging on
to a whorish ole lie
and how is it that
we are goin to EVOLVE
BLACKER, into a NATION
                              if

we can't even tell our
CHILDREN
we don't celebrate farts no mo.

Voodoo On the un-assing of janis joplin :warning: to ole tom

Early one morning
    Bessie, sweeeet, Bessie
turned to
        Billie, Bird & Otis
Yeah. Bessieeee, sweeeet Bessie
        put her hands on her hips
    and let her jellyroll sliiiiip
        and said
    Goddamn it, I dun heard just
        about e-nough of that shit!
        Z O T !!!!!!

Missing Beat

as i am,

i should be able to
balance

water jugs on my head
and

move the wind to shame

      the air should roll
   back
like waves

when i pass
my footsteps should

cause the earth to
        rumble

    but as i am

as we are
      i have lost heat
      have been too far

too long
from the sun's beat

     the vibrations of my

      black bones are un strungggggggg
    are not universal/unified
           anymore

    as i am,

(and it is rhythm to some)

i can only bougaloo & bop

Proclamation/From Sleep, Arise

we go back
to who we were
the slave period is over
        is over
           we go back
              go back

to be who we were
    who we are

        go
        back
                forth
            come
            KINGS AND QUEENS
            THE SLAVE PERIOD IS OVER

Remember Times
for Sandy

suppose they had cheated me out of my
        Black-ness
my po ver ty, my ghet to
what would i have done/how would i have
        hated them
what beauty would i have to go back to
        WHY

on the street
4-tray & cottage grove
memories do the cha-cha
where i first got my ear burned
when i first got my hair DONE up/in/
fifty cent juju tight curls cause
mother didn't have a dollar for
shirley temples. yeahhh.

on the street of 47th where i
was picked girlfriend number three
by prettyboy and june bug caught t.b.
and died and we went to the pershing ballroom
the night of the funeral and jammed and cried
oh—and

the neckbones every sat. with mustard and turnip
greens and sweet potatoes and cornbread
and the a.m.e. church on 46th & evans where
everybody was in the missionaries and young peoples
choir with maroon bottoms and white tops
and catch a girl kiss a girl under the
church steps and Betty Jean stayed too long
but she was fast anyway and her sister Dotty
was too and wore brown horn rimmed glasses
and they mama had a gold capped tooth.

Supposed I had been robbed/snatched
out of Drexel Park on tuesday or thursday evening
after choir rehearsal with the soft summer wind
blowing "the boys on my streets" Oh-Rig-I-NAL
version   du-wahhhh   du-wahhhh
Baby, Baby, wind wind blowohoh wind wind blowohoh lawd
first infatuation with
shoe string necktie wearers and earth angel moaners

oh the pain of being alive, a nervy black with so
much eyes and lips and shiney nose
and hair sticking up and touched up edges
where could the heart hide that beat SO LOUDDDDDDDD
everytime a **** boy **** came to my house
(and mother said) bop but don't two-step up inheah . . .
    SUPPOSE I HAD BEEN DENIED
waistline parties, basement grinds with the ** boys ** trying to
        push you into a corner or roll with you
            in de middle of de floor!
    like work wid me annie uh huh uh huh i say
        work wid me annnnnnnniiiieeeee. lets git it while
            the gittin is gooddddddddd

(so good so good)

SUPPOSING I HAD MISSED
    the dramatic classes at the Lucases who
    only picked the lightest ones for the
    heaviest parts and my mother
        SPOTLIGHTING
    her little Black wick in a YELLOW (look out i'm
        coming) dress
        with brown & white oxfords and white socks!
       and YELLOw ribbons
i might have looked pretty
being so brown such a brown vaseline nadinola child
  i MIGHT have been pretty, mama's bowlegged BABY . . .

        But the lessons were clear
        from then on in

        Talk. Proper. Speak. Softly. ALWAYS sound yo
        S'ssss & T'tttttt.

until (whispers whispers) "Estelle's kid talk like white folks."

        The be-ginning of the end of love?
          Naw. It was too late.
11 years. Going on twelve.
And I would always remember
        Times.

Somebody Call
(for help)

    i remember the night
    he beat
    her
    we all heard her scream
    him break some glass
    her beg
    dont do it

the hit
imagined the cut
heard the door open
her running running running
in the hall   way
                              screaming blood blood

saw bloods
in my head
would not open
my door
the po-lees came   (some body called)
say who cut de ladi
in de mouth who put her out
wid no coat no shoes
                              (some body called
                                      some body called   for help)

heard the pigs take her
                              take him
                                      away
beat HIM he beat HER beat HIM down the stairs

heard HIM call
                  (for help)

no   body opened they door.

next morning
there was
this blood
on the walls
see
little smudges here there
from hand from mouth (no doubt)
running running along the walls in splatters in sblobs
running running

                  i could wipe the stains away
                  i could do that i could
                  but i thought (surely)
        (4 days past)

          someone (else) would have
          (why) the janitor
          empties the garbage
          mops the hall   way floors
               every   dayyyy

      but

          HE   DON'T TOUCH THAT BLOOD!
MUST be because he don't
hear her screaaaammmmming
do he don't he need to ERASE that blood   runningstill   still

      on the walls   the second floors   first floors   allOVAH

                    BLOODSssss
          RUNNING RUNNING RUNNING
          against the walls

                    BLOODSssss

          RUNNING RUNNING RUNNING
          in hall ways

                    BLOODDDSSS
          RUNNING   RUNNING   RUNNING

          THROUGHOUT THE WORLD

      CUT*TING IN*TO EACH OTHER

                    some   body   (pleeease)

          CALL

               for help)

Look at My Face
a collage

It was the beginning of me
once more, inside my skin,
                     between my bones
I curled and grew
               nude
oh and my tears cupped with
the palms of my lids
                  it was the beginning
and was mist waving and ticking
through the air
each step fell me, rolling
falling falling rolling
                     but oh
bits of me splintered in to a mirror
falling falling rolling,
                     in . . .

setting/slow drag

i would like to scream but there is no one to hear. here. i have already spent several days crying time.

i would like to sleep but i have worn sleeping out. and then, i have
no pleasant thoughts to lullaby.

i have lined up all my bottles of pills and counted them and calcu-
lated what i could do with them with my self. i have acknowledged
that i am a coward since i have, before, gotten as far as the lining
and counting but have never even taken them out of their bottles.
i can not do it . . .

     i/find/my/self; i hear my own audience, imagining
how it would all sound to say that she slept herself away.

if i could be around to hear how well the trip would come
off.
if i could lay death on me like a piece of clothing, if i
could convince myself that it is like sleeping sweet dreams,
forever, which i could like a lot.

But it is just that i wouldn't have a chance
To make a mistake.

       i don't know who i am.

i've been tricked. someone stole me and left who in her place. the
body looks the same but i'm not fooled by   similarities.
i know the difference between me and somebody else.

   (LeRoi and some others too/i have tasted the blood on the pages)

We grew in.

    And now—

Nothing is sacred except the exploitation of one's soul.
We always find out too late.
i am writing like this because this is the only way/if you will get
into my head you will know this better.

         to reach a state of holiness
         you have to not have a t.v.
         refuse to turn on the radio
         and put 'trane on a box, often.

         if you do not have a box
         you could listen to the
         sounds in your head and
         then go find a box and
         hear 'Trane (no, not with
         your ears) this

         will make you shout. holiness. the ghost

to be holy is to be lonely, i think, & remember and return to the
sun.

       one must generally write specifically about self.

the secret self, dreaming writhing hidden hiding
self, softer than the babe and more lasting than, forever

and then to think one's soul mediocre . . .

                    i never meant to be a writer
                    must i still account?

You will be different if you stay alone a lot.
You will speak in tongues.
                    Yes, i believe in something
                    it is the total unstopping/is
                    the ultimate reality is insanity spaceality
                          cos-mo-lity
            If you really want to read about Blackness
                  look at my face . . .
i am thinking about all the fat people.
i am thinking about all the steel outside
i am thinking about the boy who lived in the Y who went crazy
3 days ago.
i am thinking about a drunk who didn't move faster than a silver
t-bird.

i am thinking about not thinking.
play/stage directions/blues
perhaps it should be clear why i am here. but,
perhaps it should be clear why i am here. i said,
        have you ever heard of your self?

i would not walk until i was two, but i scooted backwards and
talked
a lot made sentences and could remember things. they said.

perhaps it should be clear why i am here.

how many times have you answered your self today and smelled
your own breath?

have you ever looked at your self as if you were somebody else?

perhaps it should be clear why i am here.

i have been thinking of a world i can't think of.

perhaps you don't think i hang together.

suppose you try me and see how you do.

perhaps it should be clear why i am here.

stretch or color or break your mirror.

have you ever wanted to tape record your mind on the wind
or sing in 4 part harmony with the rain like du-wahhhhhh.
                              fog is eternity . . .

have you ever looked at somebody else as if he was you?

                    i am trying to tell you the truth.
                    i am dying to tell you a lie.
                    i am hoping you will see or hear.

i am thinking about not thinking . . .

perhaps it should be clear why i am here.

The Story/Riff

the story is about yesterday. this story is about what tomorrow was
like yesterday. this dream is about the time that got lost when the
clock stopped next month. this story is about the little girl who put
on the wrong pair of feet when she got up out of the toilet and
went to the wrong system and her church got cold ribbons.

this story is about the little girl who wanted to sing to the world
and went to the garbage can, but everyday she opened her mouth
to get her dirt her wind went astray and she vomited hate. This is
about the little girl who died on her way to the world.

this story is about the nappy-headed little nigguh who wanted to be
hell but he had snot in his eyes and couldn't lace up his hurt and
got kicked out of his space by the time before kindergarden.

this is a story about the moon being colored and singing the blues
and russia firing on it and spitting on south jesus.

this is a story about a mountain is in my mind has a skin problem and thinks it is a tree beside years changing leaves, it keeps on growing.

this is a story about a cigarette that wouldn't smoke because the numbers man kept telling it it would grow up to be cancer. and it did and the numbers and cancer got married.

this is a story about a la-dy who put a dirty blanket on a cold dead man who forgot he was dead when he smelled the grape and moved earth with his wine bottle.

this is a story about a wino i know who has black skin and purple lips and hair bumps on his teeth and shits camus.

this is a story about a world that gave itself up to people/blew it to bits got busted and fucked and overcame freedom.

this is a story about the wind forgetting the melody and riffin fuh days, blowing our minds into harmony we forget how to end how to end how to

perhaps it is clear why i am here

this is a story, to fit a world.

Poem/Ditty-Bop

Caw, Caw, Caw . . .

Have you ever been in love?
Have you ever been in love?

The way you walk is good to me.
The way you talk is good to me.
Have you ever been in love?
The way you do anything is good to me
You could be magic, blue to black magic,
magic is you.

Have you ever seen love?
Have you ever seen your face?

You could be magic, blue to black magic,
magic is you.

Have you ever been in love?
Have you ever been love?
We could be magic, magic is us,
Let's grow in love.

And While We Are Waiting

and while we are waiting

   for the ashes of the evil

to kiss the soles of our feet
and caress our eyes in pyramids of dust

   yes, while we are waiting,

         for the sun to cover/kiss the night
         our faces and limbs sweating honey

and while we are waiting and
             wishing and
             needing and
             dying and
             living in spite of

oh, while we are waiting
let us work and build and lasso
the universe with our spirit and
above all things,
while we are waiting . . .

let us love

JAMES CUNNINGHAM

A Welcome for Etheridge

I don't pretend to drink
openly on the street
from my intangible glass
dripping spirits on the ground

nor do I toss
mere words against the wind
like welcome bro. knight
and expect them
to endure
as stubbornly
as hardened glass
shattering
against this alley wall

nor sound
one half as loud

I don't pretend to drink
openly on the street
but your being home
cries out
for something like that . . .

The City Rises

the city rises
a sad stiff wooden place
where everyday
it rains
on someone's love
and storms away with glass smashing noise.

the city rises
as it hangs another injured head
upon a lean indifferent tree.

the city rises
with sad stiff wooden coughing sounds
rises
as only stunted structures can.

St. Julien's Eve:
For Dennis Cross

brahms
stabbed me in the ear
till I could only hear visible things
like patterns moving
on a lip
or falling away like ashes

or something dry & juicy beyond the teeth
like gleaming sun & stuffed clouds
trapped in mid-air
at midnight

who?
assaults me now
besides
the wind-man tearing at the bridge
where rufus stands
cursing at the sky
until he too falls away
like his falling shoe

why does the river
float up to the sky
where you are standing in a boat
between the water & the moon

where you have dropped your anchor
in the freezing cold

it's your turn to stab me—
this time in the eyes
& on the fingers
straining to grasp

the invisible things
arming themselves
in your throat

Incidental Pieces to a Walk :
for Conrad

they
say
you
went
abroad

some
say
you'll
stay

a sister
swears
she
saw
a
shadow

another
swears
a
whisper

a
brother

swears
he
heard
a
step

I
swear
nothing

For Cal

a sandstone carriage
near a lake
bitter as a lemon
sweeps four wheels
across my lips
where housewives
whisper over coffee
with their falling teeth

I could whisper too
about the honey
sticking to their hair
let down at night
like weeping.
about the war

that's ended
with a silence
and nowhere to go
but to the carriage
near the lake
where there're no roadsigns
and no homes
and no more notions
bout being too proud
or beautiful
to die in public
or in the rain.

Rapping Along with Ronda Davis

1.

Moon beams & yams
play about your mouth
and I'm hungry
hungry

to
rise
hard

to
touch
you

from the in-side

2.

banging like
water
up against a rock
I'm
at
your door

so
come

on tip toe
softer
than
the
moon
that's out of place
until
it enters
through
the door

                    hot & stiff
                    lost
                    & half-delirious
                    embedded & gleaming
                    deeper than Sampson
                    stranded
                    among your hair.

A Street in Kaufman-ville:
or a note thrown to carolyn from rodgers place

I.

ripley or not

There are madmen
who worship

doris day
or make believe

a leaner face
a bigger ass
or darker hair

at any rate
the drooping arms
of something younger
or less straight
less severe
or less determined always
to smile

at REAL trouble

a madness unlike my own
who
looks with a hope-laden ear
and if there's music

falls madly in love
with the song.

madness follows me
like a straight question
or like the female wind that blows men up.

come
        help me gather my debris

II.

bob's hustle-shop

if only I could answer you . . .
tell you how much fragments really weigh.

if only lone sharks fed a solitary broken hand or two upon the scales

like butchers do . . .

Solitary Visions of a Kaufmanoid
(:bob kaufman : a san fran cisco kid)

        bob-ing split-able heads
        feeling buoyant and teasing
        short lame-footed snails
        dreaming of dishwater
        and left-over shark

        (served in pale dishes)

        and late at night.

        a sea-witch whore
        minus visible fins
        ignored even my visible charms:
                        I'll make YOU a proposition—
                                (kiss my ass!

        but I had lena on record
        and what is there to say for a song

a record that turned and tossed for company
(all night long)

and as I slumber
comfort the lone survivor
in my will:

tan/fastic lotion/dreams
for the sun
lost in a pale orbit

somewhere
                (late at night)

Lee-ers of Hew
(From a Trio for Don, for Bro. Lee)

slurped
and waters moved
grinning with lotus-shine

laughed at shadows growing small
as unsmiling wrinkles on a thumb
steady as bongo scales we moved
swift as riverbeds
scented with stillness and yellowing leaves

trickled
and stirred ourselves like desert swans
plunging into space
where dolphy tosses
while eric fires the engines
of his midnight trane
and andrew places fingers in the flames

a
drift
upward in a blaze
singeing
the nile

the drift toward
murder

      or suicide
while

      shadows moan in idleness

arms drifting everywhere
the unstarched sleeves rolled up for slaughter

From the Narrator's Trance

6

a song thumbed down a cruiser for a ride
along huge alto-chested bars
and as the curtain stirred
became unaware of any music

driven through the beautiful black center of a scale
the steering alto horns began to move
and the curtain stirred

large looping ear drums
darker than nina's neck
or a charge plated high
winked at the brother
in the bass player's gown of swift blue notes
more incredible than earth
clinging
round the bar of G SCREAMING
like an interrupted trance.

7

there were blood spots on the skirt
the priestess wore

she had no other sacred duty than to sing
while keeping time

while leaping up the scales
as bearded brothers shouted down

had no other sacred duty than to dance
while finger popping juicy layers with the curve of a knife
that fell down suddenly
shouting and screaming
some sip incense
to forget

swahili
moaned against her throat
and whispered
click songs
made like auction blocks

in a thousand keys
that bared her legs
like secret windings in the wind

or long armed emirs
beating skins waxed by night
the birds came crying

oluto

8

and birds came crying
out of sleep

fooooooooooooooooooga
                fooooooooooooooooooon ga

praise
oluto

aaaaaaaaaaaaaaaaaaaaah
nnnn nooo nunga

nnnnnnnnnnnnng aaa

9

the woods are overhead   over everywhere

praise be oluto

the woods drop choruses like rain

oluto smiles and everywhere
I am turning
into
the god oluto

the woods murmur swahili tones
which go on rising
as we leap
like crying bridges stretching into night

be birds oluto
leap and flow like torrents
bursting into flames where spear drums float

restless as sperm-clouds

oluto
oluto
aaaaaaaaaaaaaaaaaaaah

Slow Riff for Billy

The setting
had no special theme
no privacy
for night
or early noon
no urge
to sing
or stroll
in wonder at the air
but still
he ventured forth
stroking an eyelash
and a rose
and dripping powder

with his smile
moved
without even knowing
the shape
that sagged before him
on the branch
moving as blossoms do
fading with each step
and as the branch snapped
he stood there screaming
for small boats
gliding through the air
for smells of unfried apples still in bloom
for huge ferocious stars.

A Plea to My Sister
Carolyn Cunningham: the Artist

in the kitchen
making dishes with a brush

dressing/pressing something down
in blinking pastel/oils
on black velour
where flame-shades fire
from eye to eye
over a bridge
or a melting wall

just blown down or up
a solitary nostril's arc
or some unknown region
on le roi's face

they dig your work
paint me

as though we were 21
&

free self-liberated minds
thinking in black and other proper shades
moving cross a bridge as easily as air
instead of taking hamlet's stingy steps
or walking like ghosts
unsure of their directions
                    (new or old

are you pleased with the view
with only hyde park
standing
proxy
for
your
promised land
                moses
are you pleased?

why you can lift me!
        (where do women get such strength?

as easily as a brush
as though I weren't a door
between two worlds

swinging like mad stone veils
stirring on your cuff
or don's dai shiki sleeve

stirring like pages coming loose
and scattering paper soul
or the cat's milk on carolyn rodger's bed

but while I'm in here touching things
like the softness
on a statue's cheek

paint me

paint them/us/theirs as some breathless part of me
lying dead
and without anything to drink
or wet my lips

frightened like soul dust
pausing on the ledge
like a lingering breath

lying dead
along the road
my sides are splitting me
        (it's no joke)

to die along the road
and wait

depending on brothers
listening for their steps
making summertime foot prints
of children laughing

        all the while
they know

a foot step is a fickle thing at best

like brothers wearing black
or only proper shades of it.

or unforgiving filigree clamped tight or loose
on Afro heads

I know a sister who likes to cook
and waits beside her open door
just to feed a brother

a brother unlike me
just back from the bath room
where I've been really dealing with the man

is she still waiting?
waiting with her pressing comb still warm
and her simple willingness to cook.

paint me

From a Brother
Dreaming in the Rye
(for Don)

Touch
is what the eyes do, sometimes
and sleep a habit fingers have,
or even feet, pursued in dreams.
running from a man who wants to stop
to put a record on
who wants to dance and shout and preach
that God's a goddamned lie
and if you think he ain't
just step outside.
and on and on and on we run
but feet are more prepared than I
for what's expected in a dream,
and so they fall asleep,
and soon I'm down and eyes
are crushing me, and even hands
are pounding metal out of me,
and even worthless minerals like bone
no pawn broker would glance at twice.
and only my ears leap to my defense
poking me inside my head,
the part that's not been leveled yet—
leveled like my once proud nose
whose vanished heights glare at the place
where I lie fallen, as his words
crush down like concrete things
with but one chilling thought in mind:
I oughta kill your ass.
You almost made me lose my beat.

The Covenant
(for Don)

Let us stiffen
into metal
into blades
and cut

the less than invisible wire
that pulls our people
back and forth

to work
at emptiness
at confusion
at madness
back and forth
and day by day.

Let us melt
into the wind
and wreck the slave ships
as they set out once more
to our destruction
night and day.

Into thunder
while they
are still like trees
unbending
in the wind
of what is new
and brings new life
and new awareness
of ourselves.

Let us move
while they
are bathing
at the beach
with great white robot limbs

and robot minds
and robot ease.

Let us loose the cymbals
of our strength
striking
in accord

at their heads
at their feet
at their hands
at their backs
fingers and daggers at their throats

till they come home
where humans live
and leave their space suits
buried in the sand.

A Footnote
to a Gray Bird's Pause

Who are we to love
with so much weight of
stillness and trembling and
laughter. With so much darkness
in the eyes and on the lips
and on the hands. Who are
we?

I will be constant as
the rain that glides slowly
down my skin. And just as
silent till I feel a heaviness of
need to look and touch and
even laugh with you, and tell
you things.

Or only tell them to myself

as I gaze motionless at
the tilting flight of birds,
and when I do move, merely
toss small rocky thoughts into the lake

There is no better proof of
living, than this love, no better
place to love than here in this
gray world where common birds
tilt their wings and drop their
droppings on the rocks, and rain
glides slowly down.

While Cecil Snores:
Mom Drinks Cold Milk

the red carpet-ing
led up to steps
wandering swiftly past
the gaping mezzz
aaa
    nneeennn
where
leon
    tunes
could have been singing
if
sidney
hadn't floated to the screen.

the picture was the same
only the clothes were different

the flame-ground surface
        underfoot

then ushered me
    over

to a seat
after changing into
an invisible chair
cushioned by a darkness
sad and indistinct
and arbitrary

like an upholstered shadow
would never
be genuinely blue

like the space outside
and overhead
and in a sad bright
black boy's eyes
who
never
knew
his
dad
among all the oppressors that he saw

I sat there puzzled
by a movement
on my skin
inchworms on greensleeves
tremble
up my arm
into the light
where I am wearing red
and
the screen
is
flat like silver
and dull
as grey

grey
as any black boy's eyes
who
must

look
among the oppressors for his dad.

Leg-acy of a Blue Capricorn
(for Bro. James Mosley)

1.

said
a hip/lip-ful
as his gapped teeth
began to rap
like hard smooth knuckles
     truth
   the
on

a preacher's son
still he died
in noisy gold pants
unlike his father

   art(of making it
who

at any compromising thing

sealing the eyes of death
with blue wax.

2.

I sat lost
and confined on the bus.
the window was closed
to the sun dangling
outside a non-combustible thread
I rubbed against
the glass with
my last finger.

I sat hungering
for a woman
who invented jelly
to spread some

on my slick head
hanging in mock solitude
like some bewildered insect
wondering
        what's left?
after gray stones
            and green trees
                    have gone

Happy Day
(or Independence Day)

when I get to heaven
gonna be
right down here on earth
when I get to when
I get to
gonna be right
gonna feeeel right
right down here on earth
o happy day
when we look for a heaven
right down here
on
a
black
man's earth

gonna feel alllll right
down here
on a black man's earth

gonna feel
gonna feel like shouting
gonna feel
gonna feel like killing—time—till
that happy day

right down
gonna feel like dancing
right down
gonna dance me a war
right down
right down here
right down
right down here
gonna do me some shouting
right
right
right down
right down here

High-cool/2

the cop
with a cold
with his cold shadow dead
beside him
needs no medicine

Tambourine

hear me
don't you hear me

ain't going nowhere
till you do
till you hear me
calling you

calling you brother
calling you
calling you sister
calling you
yeah calling you old folks
calling you

come on home
come on
where there's a brand new Bible
for saving you

come on
can't you hear me?
ain't going nowhere
till you do

Incest for Brothers: A Criticism

Although it might not sound like it, what is about to spill from this unwieldy pen of mine is nothing less than an affectionate love offering ("Let us be clear, we've got to have an undying love for our people!") and though it may sound like multiple incest to say so, it is addressed to a couple of brothers with the names of Calvin and Eldridge. What have they been up to lately to cause the ink in my pen to behave with so much concern for their sakes? They have written two very formidable collections of essays in which they both attempt to take on the ol' man, himself. And all because of Uncle Richard and their very own self-adopted Uncle Mailer. Of course, I've always suspected Calvin of not being a whole brother, but I've always resisted such un-brotherly misgivings in the interest of showing due respect for our common mother and our common heritage: the Black American experience we share.

I don't mean to brag, of course, but even when we were kids, I used to warn Calvin that if he persisted in his underhanded ways, he'd surely grow up to be a peeping Tom. He even went to an academy for pseudo-psychologists to tighten up his game. But it was our own fairy-godmother who really had the most influence on my two brothers. According to our grandmother, this fairy creature had predicted that though all of us would grow into conscious black writers, two of us were doomed to being poor black readers. But a rival fairy from Ofay Uncle Mailer's side of the fence was able to soften the curse by allowing for one little modification: she granted the ability to track down the central passages on a page, but she was helpless to prevent poor doomed black distorting eyes from taking over during a closer reading.

Now it should be pointed out, in all fairness, that there is considerable family pride among us; consequently, we're always talking about our parents, especially our ol' man, from whom we take most of our traits of style and subject matter. In fact, it is really in terms of the common themes we toss about that our family resemblance can be best observed—themes like color, self-esteem and manhood. I have made conscientious attempts to grow away from all this, but Calvin and Eldridge are still formidable name callers.

Perhaps, if our father hadn't left so formidable a legacy, we might not be so bent upon fratricide. But he did, and like the father in the ancient Jataka tale, made the mistake of giving us our disturbing share before actually departing, only to be vilified by two of the very sons whose independent means came from his very own loins. Just one of those bitter paradoxes, I suppose.

Calvin, surprisingly enough, has more family pride, in one sense, than any of us, for his pride is as deep as his curiosity. That's why when he finally gets around, in his writings, to the subject of the ol' man, he is not content to look under just *his* garments, but insists on opening our grandfather's closet as well. And while he is in the bedroom where the closet is, he never fails to be overtaken like some Hamlet-scholar by his own loud fantasy life in which grandfathers, uncles, and cousins alike are thrashing mightily in the bed.

But what might a person see if he were not at the mercy of, if he were not hampered and handicapped by Brother Calvin's peeping Tom imagination, and his poor, heavy pitch black eyesight? What I know of us Baldwins, Grandfather, no less than Uncle Richard, is a knowledge that has nothing to do with Calvin's fantasy pages, littered as they are with various soft-bodied hermit crabs and other creatures that live only in empty shells, or with large groups of wading birds that thrive on long necks and long legs, and long post-Freudian tapered bills as they dig in the mud along marshes and river banks. This fantasyland of Brother Hernton is littered with pages that feature just such curiosities. But to dwell there is to seclude oneself from any significant literary comment; though not too far away, one can always hear the butchering sounds of Eldridge's cleaver. But at least the brilliant edges of his hack work do not drip with insincerity. His integrity is as stainless as his blade. He is *very* sincere. We need only consider his title: *Soul On Ice.* What other qualifications does a butcher need?

Whatever else you might call Cleaver, he's not to be confused with that peeping-Tom pimp of a Brother Hernton. Why do I call him a pimp as well as a peeping-Tom? Simply because the book in which he attacks Baldwin, under cover of a so-called analysis, bears the title: *White Papers for White Americans,* and the essay in which he pulls his job is called "Blood of the Lamb." How is he being a pimp in this essay? Certainly not by merely moving his words about so that they beg and distort point after point in his ghostly wanderings through Baldwin and Wright (Why ghostly wanderings? He hardly touches a single real point, he simply loiters in the neighborhood of substance). No, what makes him a pimp is simply the fact that his discussion of Baldwin and Wright is no more than so much meat that he is offering to the already swelling white market for sensationalism that he, himself, accuses the civil rights movement of catering to.

Yes, my brothers have personal difficulties—over the matter of sex. I must confess: they are both heterosexuals. Of course, that's no problem in itself, but you see, like color, they think it matters. They think love comes with fewer difficulties that way, with fewer unpredictable things to bear. What is a man? What is manhood? The respective answers of Hernton and Cleaver are the same. In fact, they labor under the same adolescent conception that causes the father of David in *Giovanni's Room* to be so baffled and inadequate a father. He and my two brothers think that to be a man is to be a bull. And what is a bull?: the same thing that Clayton Riley, in the *Liberator* (Dec. '67), associates with the white hippies and their concept of a spade:

> The biggest dupes in the carnival are those Blacks who by some perverted logic imagine themselves caught in the same bag as their disturbed Hippie "pals." The East Village "Spade" in this age of sexual emancipation is identifiable by nothing more than his "revered" image: that of phallic toy, a primed wellspring of lust who roams the downtown streets as a thoroughly noble savage.

It is just this aspect of the hippie's psychology that Baldwin (*Nobody Knows My Name*, "The Black Boy Looks at the White Boy") has in mind when he expresses his own bafflement over Norman Mailer's *The White Negro*:

> the great gap between Norman's state and my own had a terrible effect on our relationship for it inevitably connected, not to say collided with that myth of the sexuality of Negroes which Norman, like so many others, refuses to give up. The sexual battleground, if I may call it that, is really the same for everyone; and I, at this point, was just about to be carried off the battleground on my shield, if anyone could find it; so how could I play, in any way whatsoever, the noble savage.

And further on in the essay, Baldwin enlarges on his objections to

Mailer's view of black experience, and at the same time connects Mailer's vision to that of Hippiedom:

> Both *The Naked and The Dead* and (for the most part) *Barbary Shore* are written in a lean, spare, muscular prose which accomplishes almost exactly what it sets out to do. Even *Barbary Shore* . . . never becomes as downright impenetrable as *The White Negro* does.

Now, much of this, I told myself, had to do with my resistance to the title, and with a kind of fury that so antique a vision of the blacks should, at this late hour, and in so many borrowed heirlooms, be stepping off the A train. But I was also baffled by the passion with which Norman appeared to be imitating so many people inferior to himself, i.e., Kerouac, and all the other Suzuki rhythm boys. From them, indeed, I expected nothing more than their pablum-clogged cries of *Kicks!* and *Holy!* It seemed very clear to me that their glorification of the orgasm was but a way of avoiding all the terrors of life and love.

All the terrors of life and love! Avoid them and what happens? You cannot be a man. You cannot be a man anymore than you can be an artist for it takes a man to be an artist. To be an artist, to be a writer, requires that you force yourself to examine, to face and to change yourself, and through yourself, reality; it requires the ability and the willingness to face life, and to make an effort to deal with whatever you find there. And this is because another version of the writer's task is simply the notion of maturity. This version is embodied in the story of Eden as Baldwin interprets it ("As Much of the Truth as One Can Bear," *Opinions & Perspectives from The New York Times Book Review*):

> I am a preacher's son. I beg you to remember the proper name of that troubling tree in Eden: it is "the tree of the knowledge of good and evil." What is meant by the masculine sensibility is the ability to eat the fruit of that tree, and live. What is meant by the "human condition" is that, indeed, one has no choice: eat or die. And we are slowly discovering that there are many ways to die.

This troubling tree is something that a Hernton or a Cleaver would only think of walking around, for one gets the impression that

manhood, for them both, has nothing whatever to do with knowledge: the terrible facts which are also the terrible though liberating,
mysteries of life, the beauty and power of which will remain hidden
so long as they are not looked at and into. But I could be wrong.
Perhaps it would occur to Hernton and Cleaver to do more than
merely side-step the terrible issues in Eden. They might even think
to climb the tree like school boys. The height would certainly appeal
to Hernton, who is always on the lookout for ideal peeping-Tom
posts from which to perform his literary comment, his literary name
calling, his ghostly bedroom snickering. Snickering, when he would
do well to getting down to the real business, the real opportunity in
that room: unraveling and extending the words of a dead man's
legacy: NOTHING IS EVER ESCAPED.

Cleaver's first impulse would, no doubt, be to chop it down, for it
is merely a playground fantasy-tree. But he could hardly do this
while his brother is peeping from the midst of it. But perhaps I'm
not doing my brothers full credit. The significance of the tree for
manhood need not be lost on them. The tree of manhood is simply
a device for reaching the top; the *boy* who gets there first is a *man.*
It is purely a physical thing: a physical means to the height of a
climax. That's why Bigger Thomas was more of a man than Rufus
Scott, according to Cleaver's reading. Rufus was simply a ghost who
did the white thing: he jumped off a bridge singing Patti Page's
theme song: "Why Not Take All of Me?"

This is an indication of how serious a critic a Cleaver can be,
before he takes off to Hippieland, Walt Disney's realm of the
eternal orgasm, the eternal hard. But his cleaver is so unwieldy that
he soon reaches the bottom where the source and his real hero lies:
Mickey Spillane. His poor accursed eyesight has deceived him into
thinking he has reached Richard Wright and Bigger. And the
reason for this un-brotherly mix-up is nowhere better explained than
in a passage from Baldwin's discussion of Gide ("The Male Prison",
Nobody Knows My Name:

> It is important to remember that the prison in which Gide
> struggled is not really so unique as it would certainly comfort
> us to believe, is not very different from the prison inhabited by,
> say, the heroes of Mickey Spillane. Neither can they get through

to women, which is the only reason their tommy guns have acquired such fantastic importance.

This is what Cleaver would have us believe about Bigger, that, like Spillane's heroes, his involvement with women (his sweetheart, Bessie) was not love, but fear; not sex, but violence. But who would ever dream of seeing Eldridge playing Brutus at Richard's grave? Or who would think to hear Hernton getting his kicks over Cleaver's shoulder? But it is only a game—for juveniles and adolescents who run about stooping and climbing without getting to the heart or head of anything.

JOHARI AMINI

Cromlech: A Tale

I

The darkness is quiet . . . a silence that screams and permeates this confined slice of space . . . it encloses as does death—an enwrapment of finality, a drawing toward inescapable absorption, a totalized sucking and draining of that bit which makes the thing revered as human life. And I wait . . . They have sent me back for a while, a space of time controlled, measured, and meted to the pawn, and measured and meted meticulously, with Their exactance proportionately charting the limitations of the pawn's endurance to Their expedients. I can feel the hypnotic monotony of rain falling on the edge of my darkness, incessant soft thuds vibrating through the stones, with an existence apart from mine, like the dead stones who also live, and they are both aware of me. But Theirs is an awareness in objectivity, an estrangement of the two compounds, water and stone, from a fleshed being whose existence they know has ceased. They observe my state but nothing more. The feel of the rain is close as though it were here with me . . . and yet it is outside—where the darkness is not metal and stone that closes and contains, where things yet untouched by Them still breathe and move and feel. The rain does not cleanse the darkness that covers and deludes. It is hard to think, to remember, to know I was, to know I existed there and moved and breathed and felt the covering delusion. I no longer envy Them. Life, the bit, remains to me; They walk as beings of death and hate and imbecilic monstrosity, assuming life.

157

I wonder if there are any of us left. Have I been here for weeks, months. How long. Everything blends . . . meshing together into an inscrutably opaque maze of sameness where nothing is defined, sharp. Where nothing has clarity. They have taken my perception of time in exchange for the darkness I am allowed . . . but my senses function still and cause my rending. And the pain . . . then I can taste the sweat of bittered brine and the gutted bile of myself . . . I can hear my screams as they howl in my throat and my blood as it roars and breaks in my head . . . I can smell my skin as it singes raw, and the urine, the uncontrollable flood, as it burns my flesh . . . I can see the darkness in lightning vermilions, magentas, blues, crashing through my eyes . . . I can feel the hot pain of the grille . . . I can feel, can still remember that I must not answer. They have not emptied me of my humanness even though I am left stupored, insensible . . .

My fingers recognize every stone now . . . One hundred for each of four walls, one hundred above me. Tens of stones in their rows between the corners and even the corners are silent, stolid in their mortar. Only the grille deigns to speak—the metal floor that carries me down to the questions and the pain and lifts me back to my five hundred stones and the numbness of my swollen nakedness . . . the numbness that keeps me from feeling the cold of the grille when it is done and They have sent me back and I lie alone in the pounding silence of my existence . . .

I wonder how much longer I will last . . . the numbness hides my weakness . . . I wonder how much longer it will be before I can not remember which questions I must never answer. Remembering how to respond to Them becomes more difficult . . . the pain of confusion, of abstracted nothingness, spirals in my head . . . impenetrably shadows my reason . . . Perhaps in time my grille will carry me down to the questions and the pain, and my screams will deafen me, and I will cease to be before I forget, before I cannot fight the shadows, before I utter answers of death to those who may be left outside . . .

How long will it be . . . They know . . . They can tell, and They wait. How long has it been . . . why . . . there is no answer . . . but there must be . . . The stones are silent in their obscene observing. The mortar and the rain will not hear me . . . they are deaf and refuse to answer. Did we begin to live too soon . . . a question of fantasies . . . life can only begin when it is snatched, taken . . . and the taking is present, not future as it never comes, not past as it never was . . .

I hear the hum of my grille beginning to descend . . . the cold sleek smoothness of the steel speaks. It is time again. They are waiting for me. They will prod, instruct . . . and then They will punish . . . slowly and gently the pain will come at first . . . then with more insistence . . . the heat of the lightning searing through the steel of the grille until the burning begins. The first drop . . . waiting and counting the short successive drops . . . on the eleventh the grille will stop. The dimension of space condenses as fear dissolves the solids left of me. I am there. I clutch myself and wait for the questions and the pain . . . it is easier. The darkness will speak softly now . . .

"How are you feeling, sister . . . I am your friend . . . you can talk to Me. . . ."

II

The day had been unseasonably cool for August, and as I walked to the meeting it seemed as though it were already late autumn. The chill of the air hovering over me had oppressed, even here in the Inner City, as it oppressed in the cold bleakness of deserted lakefront beaches during mid-winter. I needed to think, needed so desperately to think. Many things crowded through my mind, and having left home early I walked slowly, lethargically, allowing myself the luxury of time without rush, and the quiet of the streets too cool for children to play, if they could play now. So much had happened during the past few weeks that had to be thought out and dealt with concisely . . . about myself . . . about Dan . . . about what was happening . . . But it was difficult to sort things to the point of finding a beginning to thinking. What was happening . . . this was what caused the tumult of thoughts which insisted upon a mergence to the extent where sorting of essentials, realities, from the things that just seemed to be and had no substance, seemed impossible . . . But I had to think with clarity, to reach in and out . . . pull together fragmentations of what and where and why . . .

. . . Last summer . . . the Structure had classed our people as an alien minority and divided the country into five military zones, requiring us to wear an identifying marker . . . the starkness of fear

159

had coalesced the movement into an adhesive bulk . . . They had bestowed our differences . . . we became one of necessity . . . no more questions of identity . . . we were left without choices . . .

. . . Then winter . . . in the northeast zone . . . rebellions and reprisals which viciously demonstrated the strength of the Structure . . . Dan had speared the resistance there, had organized groups in other zones . . .

. . . And summer again . . . meetings, conferences, planning, organization . . . the sporadic demonstrations, rallies centering around outbreaks of disturbances . . . recurring developments of recurring issues . . . issues never new, never different—but the same disgorgements of the Structure that had spewed and writhed for all our generations . . . the last phase . . . They were moving toward a final solution of the problem of us . . . moving as quickly, as surely, as the lopping off of heads by the precisioned fall of a guillotine . . .

. . . It had begun . . . first Jean, then Mattie. Both had disappeared. At this point it was not a surprise. It was a nightmare becoming the tangibility which didn't fade when you awoke, leaving the haunting uncertain dread of an experience you couldn't remember. Three days had passed since Jean left home on her way to Carole's and never arrived. Carole waited for five hours and then began checking. None of us had had any contact with Jean since she left home, and we were sure she had been taken. Then, it was nearly thirty-six hours since Mattie had called me and we had been cut off. I had tried to get her back, but the line was out of order. I got in touch with Pat. We went to Mattie's apartment; the door stood open; Mattie was gone. It was here. We had tried to prepare ourselves psychologically for what we knew would be inevitable. But preparation was not like experience. This had a finality which was difficult to grasp, to accept. The dread was real . . . and there were six of us left.

For at least the past two months we had known that each of us was being kept under close surveillance. At the beginning we did not have a sudden awareness of Them—it was only gradually that one by one we began to recall seeing some particular face with increasing frequency; or, a car would be there, a car that had been noticed before. Within another two weeks other things happened. Carole had been on the beach alone early one evening preparing material for a study group when she had heard a shot—the bullet

160

going into the stack of books she had with her. And Pat, driving back to town one night from a downstate conference came too close to being run off the inside lane of the expressway into the median strip. We had spent hours trying to analyse and cull answers to the question of whether we should get out while there was still time; but, in the end it had become a choice of whether or not we could leave unfinished all that we had tried to do, being cognizant of the fact that all that could possibly be done now would be to continue with the projects underway while keeping security as tight as possible. So the decision had been made to stay and work for whatever time there was left. It was no longer a matter of life, individual life, or death . . . it was a matter of collective liberation for or extinction of a people . . .

. . . But thinking . . . a process seized by the quakings of the inescapable chaos. The tumult inside my head swelled with the wildness of a predator . . . thoughts screaked from the tensions . . . terror of the ultimate refinings . . . fires that would consume . . . and what should be done now . . . none of us knew . . . but this meeting would have to crystalize something. Whatever it would be, the direction to be taken from here had to come tonight. It must. There was no time for waiting, for conjecturing . . . perhaps not even for doing. Areas of responsibility would have to be shifted to cover the projects Jean and Mattie had worked on . . . we would have to make provision for other shifts becoming necessary . . . Up to now we had not been forced to experience the coldness of calculation in looking at each other and planning for what we would each have to do when any one of us would be taken. And the beginning came too soon . . . we were unprepared . . . entrapped . . . still with movement, life, but watched and contained . . . And there was Dan . . .

. . . We had been lovers when there was time . . . a day, perhaps two, together on the occasions when his work would bring him to the midwest zone. But more often, he would call me from wherever he was and I would fly there, to be with him for the ten or twelve hours he could break away and be with me . . . And we were always new for each other. The sameness and discoveries were new. The deeps in our loving pulled and held us while generating the life we both needed . . . his maleness . . . the strength of his being . . . warm black forged iron of his presence . . . his sureness of who he was . . . the sureness permeating everything he touched . . . the sureness absorbed me, showing me the universe . . . Those were my times of quiet and strength . . . isolated segments of blending . . . drinking the quintessence of him . . . reaching of fleshbound beings for other worlds, sensate, probing space yet to be created . . . movement spherical, limitless . . . And in each completion . . . quiet stillness of eternalness . . . and I was secured for the times I could not be with him.

. . . And then he was gone. I had watched him, from the gate, as he was shot boarding a plane for New York. And I knew that I must walk away as though he were only a stranger—removed and of no consequence to me . . . And I was alone. A void self. And the bared loneliness sliced of frozen glass and blown chipped ice. Dan was gone . . . But thinking would never help . . . loneliness still penetrated the ashes of my numbness, and this was the time he would not return. . .

As I turned the corner into Pat's street I glanced quickly down both sides, then behind me. Caution, by then, had become reflexive. I continued walking slowly the rest of the half-block to Pat's apartment building. Someone was there out of sight. I knew him. I could feel him. Or perhaps it was scent. He never approached me but he had been close enough for me to see his face at least twice before. The face was almost gentle, but unreal, as though automated. I knew that when I looked from Pat's window he would be there across the street, waiting. I had begun to form a hideous sort of attachment to him; it was as though he belonged to me malignantly. I knew he was from Intelligence. And he was playing the game with me. He watched and I waited. I waited for him to move. And sooner or later he would.

Going into the apartment building, I looked back for him. He was there, across the street. I smiled to myself, rang Pat's bell, and took out my key for her apartment. When the buzzer sounded, I opened the door and walked up the first floor landing. I unlocked Pat's door, and went in. And I can still remember a man's voice saying

"We've waited for you."

III

They did not know I heard them. I lay on the grille, gradually

162

regaining my consciousness, and listened to Them. They were talking in loud voices—voices so loud that the noise seemed to shatter my fleshless ears and expose the soft and tender parts of my brain to the roarings of a wild beast. They were not the voices which had questioned me; but as I listened I could tell that They were the ones who controlled the questioning. There was light this time—the first light I had seen since They had brought me here. It was harshly brilliant and painful, and someone was kneeling over me—someone sterile and white and antiseptically scented, and he was probing very briskly into my flesh with instruments. He prodded, and then he looked at me musingly, and delivered his opinion. He said too much was gone. He said they had ruined a good specimen, and that They should have exercised more care. He said I was too weak, and that I would not survive. They did not seem to care for his opinion. They had other specimens.

And then, when that one had gone away, the gentle automated face came and looked into mine, and smiled to itself as I had smiled to myself the last time I saw it. It looked at me with questions in its eyes, but they were questions it would never ask and I would never answer. He had followed me for weeks before They brought me here, and now he had come close for the last look we would have of each other. He said nothing to me except with his eyes, and his face became even more gentle. The tie between us was being severed now; his eyes were telling me that.

I heard Them say that I would be of no further use. It was over. I heard Them say I could be sent back up to the cell and the remains would be cleaned out in the morning. This had been the final time I had waited for, the time when the agonies of the destruction of my body would break me before I could answer Their questions.

The grille is moving, lifting me up from Them. Before long, within seconds, I will be back in my cell with my stones. The heat is gradually leaving the grille; the steel will soon be cold, as cold as the nature of the metal. The stones are as I left them. They have not changed. And they watch me from their roughened surfaces. When I am gone they will remain to observe the others who will live in this cell. And perhaps they will make comparisons, each stone in its turn, on the varying degrees of weakness to be found in the odd human species. I am numb with the familiar numbness that is always left to me when I have been returned to the cell. It will cushion my exit from this netherworld—a freeing, a passionately releasing charge of energy, relished, and executed with that aplomb inherent only in the spirit of a master, an expert in the craft and the art of the demise. I cannot see what is left of my flesh. It is better that I cannot see. That has been the one pain spared me—the pain of *seeing* what They have done. The elements of my life, the binding cohesiveness and compound of flesh, blood, bone, and soul are separated. The scent of my blood is acrid in my nostrils. It covers and stains the polished sleekness of the steel.

It is too late to think. There is no need to think . . . of Pat, Jean, Mattie. There is no need to think of Dan. No need to think of what has happened to my people. Life has gone from the earth. Only death insistently remains. Death is born, lives, grows, matures, hermaphroditically mates, and conceives death in newness, spawning itself throughout the earth, the cycle never ending but repeatedly expanding, sucking humanity downward into the eddy of extinction. The rain is still outside the stones; it is still vibrating, strumming through the wall strumming through myself. Soon the stones will no longer bind to contain me. They will let me pass through, beyond them, and I will be freed, leaving only a mass of undistinguished and indistinguishable substances for Them to dispose of. I will have cheated Them by my escape through to the cleanness of air, into the space outside these stones, becoming part of that spaciousness, refined and blended into the vapoured essence of life. All They will find will be the leavings of my shell, the castings-off, much of it dross.

* * *

There is a lightness—a weightlessness. I am separating from the shell and my weakness is voiding itself. I feel nothing but a deeply silent centre forming in the mean of my viscera—calm, frictionless, expanding, shaping, concentrating into a point as it expands—a sharp point like honed glass—and, freeing itself, exploding with one sudden burst of force . . .

. . . and as I pierced the stones, flowing through them and out into the universe, I saw again the brother from one cold night long ago walking down the center of a deserted boulevard . . . he had twisted and untwisted a flag about his neck, muttering to himself, and the golden bars choked him like a snake . . .

Childhood

    life
is at 2 playing
n a lofty room
of crumbld
walls (crumbls as pale
sweet fine as
sunsmoothed bleached
israeli
sand

    . yr sister
grows to 2
tastes crumbls (& doesn't
speak or walk
but hides
like u
behind
a gentle violated face
of marbld
eyes

    .life is at
2 aging from
crumbls crumblng
into
children's
mouths
,dying n a bilding
owned
bi
esther feldman

Brother . . .
(in reverence-celebration of the Black Peoples' Topographical Research Center)

brother
brother
liabilities are
wasted reserved on
reservations for
niggers-to-be-spaced
you are/became one
when you saw
found out the lies
had spaces
open holes
and gaped
a truth
of where you
were/are/will be
if you don't move
on/out leave to
make black life
on the land the
earth
the soil where we from

        feel
        the
        universe shudder
        pulsate
        become
        what we are
        must be
        need for life
        and movement
        brother
        move brother stream
        brother flood
        in-to the

earth
where its musics
blend become us
we spirits moving to
live to
life to create
to people the suns
of divinities

Before/and After
(which is now (& which is real)
to 1 bro. from me (to bros from sistrs)

o my brother i heard u
come through my life & face
me with a new newness. a
new newness of non/hate of
u of non/hate of yr re
flection of non/hate of me.
i heard & i could feel
yr look into me (that was
the first time (& it
touched me. saying that i
Was (i had waited cold
& long to Be.
yes.
i felt yr look & it was
life (& u were
strong. (& u
were Real.
yes.
for there were dreams be
coming. tangible. & i
could touch them &
be held.
yes.

u became the Real dream.
yes.
u talked of earthsmiles &
other things to me. &
as i watched the words u
spoke create what i
would be. as i watched yr
words make me yr/woman/
reflection. i touched into
the dream & the Real
ness of it.
yes.
u r the Real dream. but
this pome is too
long only to say that i am
still becoming what u
r. there r other words. &
longer lines. to say
that i am yr soil. come
& build here

A Sun Heals

a sun heals
as you did
when i returned
to be taken tight
for you
for you only turned
took taught
(between and against
and hard hard
hard sealing
to heal   the open openness
as the sun i remember
remember remember
the set strength

of your vulnerable man
when you sleep to
hardness resting
and resting as i watch you
sleep because you are secured
in who a man is
who controls a wo man
who controls a
terrible bursting universe
(yours i am still
and yet even though
your reflection me
is a part from its sun
(a wo man soft enough
from a nurture
of your sifting
(control me
control me for
i am and need

(Untitled)
(in commemoration of the blk/ family)

we will be no generashuns to cum for blks r
killing r.selves did u hear bros.did u hear the
killings did u hear the sounds of the killing
the raping of the urgency of r soil consuming r
own babies burned n the acid dri configurashuns
of the cycles balancing did u hear.did u hear.
hear the sounds of the balancing & checking off
checking off erasing r existence from the count
of the cosmos while r mother moans for the loss
of r funkshun & who we will never be did u hear
bros.hear .hear. hear the sounds of r mother of
her moaning as she moans while we allow her to
lie stretch ing herself from Dakar to Dar es
Salaam & she moans & tears her flesh & gushes

did u hear the gushing bros.did u hear.hear.did
u hear the sounds of the gushing oil from her
members wetly spraying the auto mated powers of
a foreign god who ruts in.to her did u hear the
sounds.sounds.bros.sounds of the rutting did u
hear.hear did u hear the rutting of the animal
with the golden hair rutting in.to her urgency
eating the sacrificed & futile fetuses erupted
n the fascinated juices of the cycles of pills
which will control the number of her mouths did
u hear. did u hear the cycles turning bros. did u
hear them we will be no mor. . . .

SHARON SCOTT

A Little More About
the Brothers and Sisters

the people know—
about what they do not have
about themselves and their children,
and also, of where they are forever not getting to
    when going—

and so, i shall never challenge you about what you think
the people might know

only about what the people are doing.

Just Taking Note—

man, them revolutionary niggers is all
    over the place—
       look life

   what's his name brother makes the trib
                every/other/day.

     they be so revolutionary like
      you know—
           moving
               moving
        in a million
                  circles.

    only seems like now, they ain't so
    revolutionary anymore.

Discovering—

i mean

   if i didn't know
   if i hadn't been   around
   or hadn't ever been   alone/

i would have really been in a trick   you know?

     waitin

       so   long.

         and

            meetin

              julia. *
*julia. a comedy/cartoon/televisionseries
about them otha blk folk—yeah?

On My Stand

i want it to be clear for us
that i am not letting it go.
        it's just not known to me
        that we can
           FEEL
                together now.

and then, i'm not sure, i can
place it in your hand, without the sweat
from mine dissolving its shell.

i am not always ready for debate
nor am i willing
to discuss at your
leisure
        the fiber of each hour.

i am not always ready for debate
debate of my thoughts, or an unlikely presence.

Okay—

"there are dreams that need rest"
        and dreamers too,
      that need to die that death
      so that they can help us now,

           to receive the darkness—
           that we can hold and see/through
           now
               and the loss
               of black blood

           in fierce and in
           watering tones.

to help us receive now,
the
Revival
the
Homecoming

over the absence of
revival meetings
and
home.

Between Me and Anyone
Who Can Understand—

i don't know about anything   sometimes
    i am not even here when i come   some moments
        i
            can't
                breathe.
                    everyone thinks i am
                    secure.
                    it must be because of a
                    certain
                    strait jacket
                        i feel.

Our Lives

No
  No
  No
        I am not doing
            my 'thing' or
            the 'thing' or
            anybody else's
                'thing'.

```
            things are
                        spots
            and spaces
                        people
            can't name,   Brothers.
```

Mama Knows

```
when i was very very
young
she told me.        then
because she thought
she could
and
i'd
forget—

that people know too hard.
and are trying to die—

that's why all our
lies and
covering over
are all so
very very
good.
```

Come on Home

```
i wonder about
the brother
who will dig
in the dirt of
```

coke cans and
old jets with
the centers
torn out   and
cigarette butts
and
spit—
in a can marked
keepchicagoclean
to—

      find a fragment
      of yesterday's
      newspaper
      which was two
      days old then
      and is two
      weeks old
      now/

         forget my wondering
         about you,   Brother!
               But— leave
               the
               dead
               noisemakers
               alone.

Oh - - - Yeah!

i would like
to make
a
brief statement
for/to
those
and myself
who think

i
can/could
ever
get rid
of my
natural.

> my nappy hair grows/lives in.   and
> lights my fire allthroughout   my
> being.

i would like
for those
who think
i
can/could
ever
get rid
of my
natural
to make
a
brief statement
for/to
me—
about what they
believe
is
themselves.

Sharon
Will be No/Where on
Nobody's Best-Selling List

nor, will anyone dare say to
her face more than once what
a boss black writer she is—
or otherwise

for there can be no recognition
for me nor my poems through
more words and more paper.
only by your

yes sister   I CAN FEEL
yes sister   I CAN HEAR
yes sister   WEWILLMOVE

Here sister, is our lives.

there can be no poems to
gratify my poems.
only changes
    action,   and steady pulses.

(then, maybe someone
can say
here was
a
heavy sister!

Salaam.

Untitled
(hi ronda)

sometimes
the poems
be
comin
so bad.
about our
beauty
about our everything
that—
sometimes
i have to
put down my pen

and
hold
their
hands.

Untitled

fisk is
a
negroid
institution
that is
trainin
runaway
black people
to
runaway
faster.   thru
un/i/ ver/shit/ tie/dumb
spacin   thru
greek/dumb
involved in
blowin my mind
for the sake
of no
namesake
so that i
may walk into the world
with a
bs
degree—

       in order to deal with fisk
       you must first deal with
       un/i/ver/sal/ i/ty
       which is the
       unitedfrontofniggasincorporated

which has nothing to do with
blackness   but.
bleakness   and
reflections from
broken mirrors
which have meant more than
seven years
of
bad luck.   fisk is
a hundred and some odd years old.

For Both of Us
at Fisk

i've ever lost were
i thought
at first
for a
long
time.
that
maybe
i'd
lose
it.

i mean—
i knew
i'd never
press
my hair but
i thought
maybe i'd
lose my mind
in
other ways
besides

madness
or. i'd
press my flesh
in your body
shirts and
brogans—

i thought maybe
i'd begin to dig
your parties—

i thought maybe
i'd lose my
blackness
here. but
i won't
'cause
the only things
i've ever lost were
mother's jewelry
dollar bills and
somebody else's
boyfriend.

       i had
a broken heart once
but it only hurt so
much because it was
still in one piece.

what i'm sayin is

you only insist upon
being called
Negroes
because
youareBLACK

you think blackness
is your nappy hair
skin coloring
and your diggin

chitterlins but.
it is your
being.
in your pores
is your blood
and your
breeding!

you can burn out
all your
hair
bury your
body
and go from
chitterlins to
caviar but
yourlifeisBLACK.

the body dies but.
the spirit moves on
from within.

BIOGRAPHIES

JOHARI, AMINI
Born February 13, 1935, Philadelphia, Pennsylvania.
B.A., Chicago State College, 1970.
Publication: Books—(Third World Press) *Images in Black, Black Essence, A Folk Fable* (folder), *Let's Go Somewhere.* Other—*Nommo, Black World, Black Arts Anthology, The Black Poets, To Gwen With Love.*
Instructor: Kennedy-King College "Mini-Campus."

WALTER BRADFORD
Born May 27, 1937, Chicago.
Education: Wilson Junior College (now Kennedy-King.)
Publication: *Nommo,* Vols. 1 and 2, *Black Expression, Black World, Chicago Daily News Panorama, Broadside Series, To Gwen With Love.*
Part-time instructor, Malcolm X Community College. Other teaching and counseling, in the field of prisoner-rehabilitation.

GWENDOLYN BROOKS
Born June 7, 1917, Topeka, Kansas.
Education: Wilson Junior College.
Publication: Books—(Harper and Row) *A Street in Bronzeville, Annie Allen,* for which she won the Pulitzer Prize in 1950, *The Bean Eaters, Selected Poems, In the Mecca, Bronzeville Boys and Girls* (children's poetry), *Maud Martha* (a novel), (Broadside Press) *Riot,* and *Family Pictures.*

CARL CLARK
Born November 21, 1932, Brinkley, Arkansas.
Education: Arkansas State College, University of Illinois
At present completing work on Ph.D. in psychology, University of Alabama.
Former science teacher, Hirsch High School in Chicago.

MIKE COOK
Born March, 1939, Chicago.
Attended the University of Chicago, University of Massachusetts.
Teaching assistant at University of Massachusetts.
Publication: *Nommo, Black Expression, Journal of Black Poetry.*

JAMES CUNNINGHAM

Born January 4, 1936, Webster Groves, Missouri.
Education: Butler University.
Publication: *Nommo, Black Voices*, Vol. 2, *To Gwen With Love*.
Book of poetry: *The Blue Narrator*.
Has taught at the University of Wisconsin in Milwaukee; is now writer-in-residence and Alain Locke instructor in literature at Cornell University.

RONDA DAVIS

Born October 31, 1940, Chicago.
Educated: Roosevelt University.
Has taught in high schools, in the Black Community of Chicago, and at the University of Wisconsin in Milwaukee.
Publication: *Nommo, Black World, Juggernaut,* and the *Broadside Series "Sister Songs."*
"Now studying black languages and the meanings of Afro-American names as related to the African concept of Nommo, the magic power of the word."

PEGGY KENNER

Born November 4, 1937, Chicago.
Education: Wilson Junior College (now Kennedy-King), Chicago Teachers' College, Roosevelt University, University of Wisconsin.

DON L. LEE

Born February 23, 1942.
Education: Wilson Junior College (now Kennedy-King), Roosevelt University.
Has taught at Columbia College, Chicago; Cornell University; Northeastern Illinois State College, and is presently instructor in Black Literature at the University of Illinois.
Books (Broadside Press): *Think Black, Black Pride, Don't Cry, Scream, We Walk the Way of the New World, Direction-score: Selected and New Poems, Dynamite Voices: Black Poets of the 1960's* (criticism). Other—*Black Arts, Nommo, Black Expression, To Gwen With Love, Black World, Journal of Black Poetry, Liberator, Muhammad Speaks, Freedomways, Chicago Defender, Broadside Series, For Malcolm, Black Poetry.*

184

LINYATTA

Says LinYatta of LinYatta: "After ten years of literary experimentation, 24-year old ex-author LinYatta has returned to the fine arts (design) and to the study of cosmic transcendence."
Publication: *Tazama, Nommo,* and *Evergreen Review.*

CAROLYN RODGERS

Born.
Birthplace, Chicago.
Education: Roosevelt University.
Publication: *Black Out Loud,* 1971, Holt and Rinehart; *Natural Process,* 1970, Hill and Wang; *We Speak As Liberators,* 1970, Dodd Mead; *To Gwen With Love,* 1971, Johnson Publishing Company; *The Roots of Black Literature; Modern Afro-American and African Writings,* Macmillan; *Night Comes Softly,* Black Dialogue Press, 1970; *Broadside Series, "Sister Songs."*
Recording: *Spectrum in Black,* 1970, Scott, Foresman and Company.
Books (Third World Press): *Paper Soul; Songs of a Blackbird, Two Love Raps* (Broadside).

SHARON SCOTT

Born April 29, 1951, Chicago.
Student, Fisk University.
Publication:*Black World, To Gwen With Love.*

SIGMONDE WIMBERLI

(Kharlos Tucker)
Born 1938.
Editor, *Black Truth,* a newspaper published on Chicago's west side.
Publication: *Ghetto Scenes,* a book of poetry; *Nommo, To Gwen With Love.*
Also writes short stories and is working on a novel.

AUTHOR-TITLE INDEX

BROADSIDE SERIES—SINGLE POEMS
50c Each ($6.00 a year)

Portfolio for Broadsides
1. Ballad of Birmingham, Dudley Randall
2. Dressed All in Pink, Dudley Randall
3. Gabriel, Robert Hayden
4. Ballad of the Free, Margaret Walker
5. The Sea Turtle and The Shark, M. B. Tolson
7. A Poem for Black Hearts, LeRoi Jones
8. Booker T. and W. E. B., Dudley Randall
9. A Child's Nightmare, Bobb Hamilton
11. Sunny, Naomi Long Madgett
12. Letter from a Wife, Carolyn Reese
14. Race Results, U.S.A., 1966, Sarah W. Fabio
15. Song of The Son, Jean Toomer
16. Back Again, Don L. Lee
17. The Black Narrator, Le Graham
18. Black Madonna, Harold Lawrence
19. The Wall, Gwendolyn Brooks
20. At That Moment, Raymond Patterson
21. 2 Poems for Black Relocation Centers, Knight
22. Not Light, Nor Bright, Nor Feathery, Danner
23. At Bay, James A. Emanuel
24. Earth, Askia Muhammad Toure'
28. Black and White, Tony Rutherford
31. T.C. (Terry Callier, True Christian), Bradford
32. Ginger Bread Mama, Doughtry Long
33. One Sided Shout-Out, Don L. Lee
35. Granny Blak Poet, Arthur Pfister
36. For Black Poets Who Think of Suicide, Knight
37. Now Ain't That Love?, Carolyn Rodgers

38. Slaughterhouse, Helen Pulliam
39. County Jail, Jill Witherspoon
40. Rip-Off, Ronda Davis
41. All I Gotta Do, Nikki Giovanni
42. Goodnight, Paula Alexander
43. Muslim Men, Sterling Plumpp
44. Long Rap, Carolyn Rodgers
45. The Nigger Cycle, K. A. Mwandishe
46. A Simple Poem To Mae, O. K .Tarajia
47. Black Henry, Rockie Taylor
48. Two Poems, Robert Keeby & Stephany
49. Tears and Kisses, J. Amaker, G. Gracia, P. Kirk-
wood, L. Lunford, & W. Rutledge, Jr.
50. For H. W. Fuller, Carolyn Rodgers
51. Poems, Bobb Hamilton, George Buggs
52. Poems, Yusuf, J. Smith, R. Bowen, C. Clemmons
53. Poems, H. Kinamo, L. Tolbert, B. Rogers,
A. Kingcade
54. Poems, L. Riley, T. Washington, Jr., Robert. L.,
M. Khalilmalik
55. Black Song, J. D. Perry
56. Black Gifts for a Black Child, Shango
57. Gonna Free Him, Evelyn Clarke
58. Three Poems, Carl Carter
59. A Hip Tale in the Death Style, J. Amini
60. Five Poems, Alice Walker
61. Four Poems, J. P. Randall, R. Oxford, J. Forsh
62. Green Apples, Dudley Randall

BROADSIDE VOICES

Broadside Album: Rappin' and Readin', by Don L. Lee $5.00
Broadside on Broadway: Seven Poets Read (cassette) 5.00
Tapes of poets reading their own books (reels and cassettes) 5.00

Tapes by Emanuel, Giovanni, Jeffers, Hodges, Knight, Randall, Arnez & Murphy, Sanchez, Eckels, Marvin X, Stephany, Lee, Kgositsile, Walker, Danner, Brooks, Major

---

BROADSIDE POSTERS

1. For Black Poets Who Think of Suicide, by Etheridge Knight; illus. by Talita Long $1.00
2. On Getting a Natural, by Dudley Randall; illus. by Leonard Baskin 1.00
   (50 signed by poet and artist) each 10.00
3. Black Silhouette, by Pat Whitsitt 1.00
4. Angela, by Talita Long 1.00
5. Protect the Sister, by Reginald Payne & Pearl Eckles 2.00

THE BLACK POSITION—A PERIODICAL (Annual) $1.00

BROADSIDE POETS

Against the Blues, by Alvin Aubert. 0-910296-73-1 .... paper $1.50

Aloneness (children's), by Gwendolyn Brooks. .... Cloth 0-910296-75-8 $3.00 paper 0-910296-55-3 1.00

Beer Cans, Bullets, Things & Pieces, by Arthur Pfister. 0-910296--29-4 .... 1.25

Black Arts: An Anthology of Black Creations, Edited by Ahmed Alhamisi and Harun Kofi Wangara.
(Black Arts Publications) 910296-06-5 .... 3.50

Black Feeling, Black Talk, by Nikki Giovanni. 910296-31-6 .... 1.00

Black Judgement, by Nikki Giovanni. 910296-07-3 .... 1.50

Black Love Black Hope, by Doughtry Long. 0-910296-20-0 .... 1.00

Black Man Listen, by Marvin X. 910296-08-1 .... tape $5.00, book 1.00
Poems and Proverbs voice the philosophy of the Nation of Islam.

Black Poetry: A Supplement to Anthologies Which Exclude Black Poets,
Edited by Dudley Randall. 910296-09-X .... cloth $4.00, paper .95

Black Pride, by Don L. Lee. 910296-04-9 .... 1.00
The second book by the impressive young Chicago poet.

Black Velvet, by Everett Hoagland. 910296-34-0 .... 1.00

Black Wisdom, by Frenchy Jolene Hodges. 0-910296-40-5 .... tape $5.00, paper 1.00

Black Words, by Arthur Boze. 0-910296-39-1 .... paper 1.00

Blues For Mama, by John Raven. 0-910296-54-5 .... .50

The Broadside Annual, 1972, ed. Jill Witherspoon. 0-910296-77-4 .... Paper 1.00

A Broadside Treasury, 1965-1970, Edited by Gwendolyn Brooks.
cloth 0-910296-53-7 $6.00, paper 0-910296-51-0 4.00

Cities Burning, by Dudley Randall. 910296-10-3 .... tape $5.00, book 1.00
Reflects the troubled emotions and tragic events of our time.

The Cotton Club, by Clarence Major. 0-910296-62-6 .... tape $5.00, paper 1.50

Directionscore: Selected and New Poems, by Don L. Lee.
paper ISBN 0-910296-48-8 $3.75, cloth 0-910296-49-0 $6.00 Special Edition 0-910296-50-2 15.00

Don't Ask Me Who I Am, by James Randall, Jr. 910296-46-4 .... 1.00

Don't Cry, Scream, by Don L. Lee. 910296-11-1 .... tape $5.00, cloth $4.50, paper 1.50
A brilliant, devastating book by a leading young poet.

Down Nigger Paved Streets, by William A. Thigpen, Jr. 0-910296-74-X .... paper 1.00

Dynamite Voices: Black Poets of the 1960's, by Don L. Lee. ISBN 0-910296-33-2 .... 2.75

East 110th Street, by Jose-Angel Figeroa, 0-910296-53-3 .... 1.50

Family Pictures, by Gwendolyn Brooks. 910296-43-X .... tape $5.00, cloth $5.00, paper 1.00

For Malcolm: Poems on the Life and the Death of Malcolm X, Edited by Dudley Randall and
Margaret Burroughs. 910296-12-X .... cloth $4.95, paper 2.95

Frank, by Carolyn Thompson (a children's book). 910296-41-3 .... 1.00

Guerilla Warfare, by Ahmed Alhamisi. (Black Arts Publications) 1.00

Holy Ghosts, by Ahmed Akinwole Alhamisi. ...... cloth 0-910296-70-7, $4.50, paper 0-910296-38-3 1.95

Home Is Where the Soul Is, by Jon Eckels. 910296-00-6 .... tape $5.00, book 1.00
A young California poet who is together and relevant.

Homecoming, by Sonia Sanchez. 910296-05-7 .... tape $5.00, book 1.00
A passionate, earthy first book by a gifted poet.

Impressions of African Art, by Margaret Danner. 910296-13-8 .... 1.00

It's A New Day (a children's book), by Sonia Sanchez. 0-910296-60-X ...... Cloth $4.00, paperback 1.25

Jump Bad: a New Chicago Anthology, Edited by Gwendolyn Brooks. 0-910296-32-2 .... paper 4.00

Life Styles, by Marion Alexander Nicholes. ISBN 0-910296-36-7 .... 1.00

More to Remember: Poems of Four Decades, by Dudley Randall. (Third World Press)
cloth 0-910296-59-6 $5.00, paper 0-910296-58-8 1.95

Moving Deep, by Stephany. 910296-18-9 .... tape $5.00, book 1.00
Love poems by a young new poet and artist.

My Blackness Is the Beauty of This Land, by Lance Jeffers. 910296-28-6 .... tape $5.00, paper 1.00

Our Business in the Streets, by Jon Eckels. ISBN 0-910296-31-6 .... paper 1.00

Panther Man, by James A. Emanuel. 910296-35-9 .... tape $5.00, paper 1.00

Poem Counterpoem, by Margaret Danner and Dudley Randall. 910296-14-6 .... tape $5.00, book 1.00
A unique arrangement of paired poems by two poets of longstanding distinction.

Poems From Prison, by Etheridge Knight. 910296-15-4 .... tape $5.00, paper 1.00

Prophets for a New Day, by Margaret Walker. 910296-21-9 .... tape $5.00, paper 1.00

Re:Creation, by Nikki Giovanni. 910296-47-2 .... tape $5.00, cloth $4.50, paper 1.50

Riot, by Gwendolyn Brooks. 910296-19-7 .... cloth $5.00, paper 1.00

A Safari of African Cooking, by Bill Odarty. ..... cloth 0-910296-72-3 $5.95, paper 0-910296-63-4 3.95

Saint Nigger, by C. E. Cannon. 0-910296-45-6 .... paper 1.00

Singing Sadness Happy, by Lyn. 0-910296-71-5 .... 1.00

Song for Nia, by Doughtry Long. 0-910296-64-2 .... paper 1.50

Spirits Unchained, by Keorapetse Kgositsile. 910296-01-4 .... tape $5.00, book 1.00

Sugarfields, by Barbara Mahone. (Distributed by Broadside Press) 1.25

The Rocks Cry Out, by Beatrice M. Murphy and Naomi L. Arnez. 910296-16-2 ... tape $5.00, book 1.00

The Treehouse and Other Poems, by James A. Emanuel. 910296-17-0 .... tape $5.00, book 1.00
Terse lyrics by widely published young poet.

Think Black, by Don L. Lee. 910296-03-0 .... 1.00

We a BaddDDD People, by Sonia Sanchez. 910296-27-8 .... tape $5.00, paper 1.50

We Don't Need No Music, by Pearl Cleage Lomax. ISBN: 0-910296-61-8; LCN: 70-156400 .... 1.00

We the Black Woman, by Femi Funmi Ifetayo. (Black Arts Publications) 1.00

We Walk the Way of the New World, by Don L. Lee. 910296-26-X .. tape $5.00, cloth $4.50, paper 1.50
Don Lee's fourth book is "softer, but louder."

The Youth Makes the Revolution, by Sonebeyatta Amungo (Black Arts Publications) 1.00

If you like this book...
you will like some of our other books listed on the inside front cover or on our flyers. You can order them conveniently by mailing this order form.

I enclose $_____ for the books listed below.
(Add 25 cents for postage and handling.)

Author	Title	Price	No. of Copies	Total

Postage and Handling _____.25

Grand Total $_____

Name_____

Address_____

City_____State_____Zip_____

Mail check or money order to
BROADSIDE PRESS
Dept. M.O., 12651 Old Mill Place   Detroit, Michigan 48238